Stephen Karcher Ph.D writes, translates and lectures on myth, divination, depth psychology and religious experience. An internationally known scholar, he has worked with *I Ching* and other divination systems for over thirty years and has produced definitive translations and commentaries as well as many scholarly articles. As co-director of the *I Ching Project* at the Eranos Foundation, he collaborated with Rudolf Ritsema to translate and produce the Eranos edition of *I Ching: The Classic Oracle of Change*. He is the author of *How to Use the I Ching, The Illustrated Encyclopedia of Divination, Ta Chuan: The Great Treatise* and *The Kuan Yin Oracle: Goddess of Compassion*, the first complete translation of a popular temple oracle.

Also by Stephen Karcher
from Time Warner Books:

Symbols of Love

Essential Shiatsu (with Yuichi Kawada)

Total I Ching

THE
KUAN YIN
ORACLE

The Voice of the
Goddess of Compassion

STEPHEN
KARCHER

A *Time Warner* Paperback

First published in Great Britain in 2001 by Little Brown
This edition published by Time Warner Paperbacks in 2003

A CIP catalogue record for this book
is available from the British Library.

ISBN 0 7515 3531 1

Typeset in Bembo by M Rules
Printed and bound in Great Britain
by Clays Ltd, St Ives plc

Time Warner Paperbacks
An imprint of
Time Warner Books UK
Brettenham House
Lancaster Place
London WC2E 7EN

www.TimeWarnerBooks.co.uk

CONTENTS

INTRODUCTION

Behind the Red Door

There is a red door just beyond the corner of this busy street in a great eastern city. For the people who live here, red is the color of happiness and luck. So even if this door is unadorned, everyone knows what is behind it. It is a temple of Kuan Yin, the Compassionate One, the One who Sees and Hears the Cries of the World. People scurry by, busy with their struggle to live, eat, love and care for a new generation.

The streets around the temple teem with greed, joy, conflict and, all too often, sudden death. In this world, where your life can change in a moment, we need a Great Protector, a *Maha Yana* we can turn to in times of fear, confusion and despair. For half the world, that protector is Kuan Yin. Wherever there are Chinese- or Japanese-speaking people, in homes, restaurants, workplaces, shipyards, small urban temples, Buddhist, Taoist and Shinto shrines and Holy Mountains, her image and her oracle are there.

Step into Kuan Yin's temple. The Buddhas of Past, Present and Future form her doorguard, for she can break the chain of karma and negative rebirth. The walls are lined with hangings and images in red and dull gold. Monkey and his companions Pigsy and Sandy, who helped the monk Tripitaka to bring scriptures to China, are there to help, for her words confer liberation. She is attended by her two disciples, the Golden Boy and Lung Nü, the Dragon King's daughter. The clouds are full of Enlightened Compassionate Beings and the air is full of incense.

There, in the corner, a black-robed Taoist priest makes an offering for a sick member of the neighborhood community that surrounds this little shrine. You drop a few coins in a bowl, take joss sticks and spirit money to burn in the Great Urn that holds the ashes of generations of offerings, and light them at an ever-burning lamp. Then you step towards the altar. Above it, Kuan Yin looks down on you out of a cloud lotus, while below her are the churning waves of the Great Ocean of Suffering. Her insightful eyes and compassionate heart wrap you in an aura of calm and joy.

Help is at hand.

You step closer and make a formal prostration. Then you pick up the *chien tung*, a black bamboo cup containing the 100 *Sticks of Fate*. These are long thin bamboo slats, red at the top and marked with a number on the hidden bottom. You whisper your question to the Goddess and shake the cup back and forth until one stick pops out. Kuan Yin has heard you and answered you.

Reading the number from the bottom of the stick, you turn to Kuan Yin's *Book of Divination*. Each number indicates a four-line Poem, a Moon Phase, a group of What Can and Cannot Happen and a set of Directions for the Wayfarer to help you focus your energy and choose the right spiritual practice. If you cannot read, the diviners will be glad to help you.

This image and the advice that surrounds it are Kuan Yin's gift of spirit, freely given in a language that all can understand. She is friendly to humans because she is a *Bodhisattva*, a Lover of Enlightenment. She was a human many times in the past and has pledged herself to an infinite expression of compassion. She will help whenever you call on her with a sincere heart. Remember her words as you leave through the red door. They will help you and guide you.

These little temples and the Goddess who inhabits them have brought solace, hope and insight to many in times of desperate need, for this ritual is an integral part of the life of tens of millions of people throughout the East. This book presents Kuan Yin's oracle as it exists in one of those temples. May it help you as it has helped so many before.

Who is Kuan Yin?

Kuan Yin is first of all a *Bodhisattva*,[1] an 'enlightenment being' pledged to universal liberation and happiness. All the many incarnations of the Buddha are *Bodhisattvas*. Early or Lesser Vehicle Buddhism maintained there was only one Buddha in any one age. Ours, the *Kaliyuga* or Iron Age, is ruled by the Buddha Sakyamuni. He spent innumerable births attaining the 'perfections' (*paramita*) needed to become Buddha, primarily wisdom (*prajna*) and selfless giving (*dana*). According to the Lesser Vehicle, very few people can walk this path. They are 'as rare as the *udumbara* blossom'.

Mahayana or Greater Vehicle Buddhism changed this. This practice began in small groups of lay people and monks who collected around the holy sites of Buddha's life. They worshiped Buddha directly and said that a path concerned only with individual salvation was a selfish path. It is meaningless to think of one person's liberation; the great compassion demands liberation for all. The only real goal is the total insight and compassion attained by the Buddha. So each person who enters a *Mahayana* life in religion begins with the Bodhisattva Vow to work tirelessly for the happiness and enlightenment of all sentient beings.

This Bodhisattva Vow is the Great Path and the Great Protector of all.

Once realized, a Bodhisattva can assume any form in any realm of being, even in the lowest circles of the burning hells, in order to help those who dwell there. The great Bodhisattvas, figures such as *Avalokitesvara, Manjushri, Maitreya* and *Ksitigarbha*, have cults and divination systems that cut across religious lines. All were once human beings like us and deeply feel for our sufferings. They have given up the hope of release from the Wheel of Birth and Death only in order to help us. Their images show their majesty, insight and infinite compassion.

The Bodhisattva's Way begins with the Vow to become a Buddha in order to work only for the happiness of all sentient beings. It unfolds and guides you to spiritual perfection over the aeons. It is expressed in two great promises: to renounce liberation and release until all beings are saved, and to transfer merit freely to others.

The path to realizing Bodhisattva nature evolves through ten stages. These steps or stages are called *bhumi*. At the seventh *bhumi*, you win enough merit to enter *nirvana* or 'no-wind', where the hot winds of desire and compulsion are forever stilled, and to move off the Wheel of Birth and Death. But your Vow constrains you. Like Kuan Yin, you choose to remain in the *samsara*, the World of Illusions, or Tomb World, we all inhabit, and work for the 'happiness of all sentient beings'. From this level on, full enlightenment is inevitable. The Bodhisattva is on the Way.

The following is one version of the ten stages or *bhumi*. We should imagine Kuan Yin as passing through all these experiences and perfections. All the names of the stages are her epithets.

- **The Joyful One**: rejoicing in the experience of *bodhi* or enlightening, the Bodhisattva perfects the skill of selfless giving (*dana*).

- **The Pure One**: perfecting herself in right living or morality (*sila*), the Bodhisattva is freed from impurities.

- **The Light-giver**: perfecting her insight into the nature of suffering and release and offering it to the world, the Bodhisattva acquires patience (*ksanti*).

- **The Radiant One**: perfecting herself in effort (*virya*) and the thirty-seven 'principles conducive to enlightenment' (*bodhipaksya dharmas*), the Bodhisattva burns away ignorance.

- **Difficult to Conquer**: perfecting herself in contemplation (*dhyana*) and the practice of the Four Noble Truths, the Bodhisattva is not easily conquered by Mara, goddess of illusion and ruler of the *samsara*.

- **Face to Face with Emptiness**: perfecting herself in transcendental wisdom (*prajna*) and insight into the doctrines of causality (*pratitya-samutpada*), the Bodhisattva now stands face to face with total release from birth and death.

- **The Far-Going One**: able to comprehend reality just as it is, the Bodhisattva perfects herself in the skillful means (*upaya*) necessary to help the myriad beings to liberation.

- **The Immovable One**: unmoved by emptiness or being, cause or non-cause, the Bodhisattva cultivates resolution (*pranidhana*) and the ability to manifest herself at all levels of existence in the time, place and form she wishes.

- **Becoming the Good**: the Bodhisattva acquires the means of analytical knowledge (*pratisamvids*) and perfects herself in strength (*bala*).

- **Cloud of the Dharma**: the Bodhisattva acquires a radiant, jeweled body through which she works miracles for the myriad beings. As space is dotted with clouds, her experience is composed of trances and concentrations. She perfects herself in knowledge (*jnana*) and obtains the ten deliverances corresponding to her vows. The process is complete and she can travel the realities at will to exercise her insight and compassion.

Kuan Yin and the Cries of the World

But for millions of people, Kuan Yin is not just *a* Bodhisattva, she is *the* Bodhisattva.[2] She is a manifestation of the most beloved figure of the Mahayana pantheon.

Avalokitesvara, the male form of this figure, is worshiped throughout Asia in innumerable forms and traditions. He is a great protector and savior who watches over the myriad beings and hears their cries, responding directly to their needs. In fact, that is the meaning of his name, *avalokita-ishvara*, the 'lord who has seen and now sees'. The Chinese form is *Kuan-tzu-tsai*, the 'one who sees the world'. Another meaning is 'she/he who hears', in Chinese *Kuan-yin*, or 'she/he who hears the cries of the world', in Chinese *Kuan-shih-yin*. These names describe a savior who hears and sees suffering and responds with potent aid.

This Bodhisattva is a human figure who, through dedication, humanity and spiritual resolution, became the Greatest of the Protectors, the *Maha-sattva*, much as Hercules became the savior of the average Greek of the classical period. The Dalai Lama, central figure in Tibetan Buddhism, is considered to be a living incarnation of Avalokitesvara, an expression of infinite compassion and insight into human suffering. From its origins in the northwest border-lands of India, the cult of Avalokitesvara spread or spontaneously arose throughout the East.

The Lotus Scripture (*Saddarmapundarika Sutra*) and the Pure Land Scripture (*Sukhavativyuha Sutra*) tell us of this Bodhisattva's life-saving powers and direct connection with the Buddha. The *Lotus Scripture* devotes a chapter to this figure, chapter twenty-five in the fourth century Chinese translation by Kumarajiva, which is often memorized and recited throughout the East. It includes the meaning of the Bodhisattva's name (Avalokitesvara, Kuan Yin or Kannon), a list of life-saving powers and the many forms in which she/he appears.

A very famous passage in the *Lotus Scripture* states that a person has only to call on Kuan Yin in a single-minded way to be saved from every conceivable calamity. Hurled into a fiery inferno, if you call on Kuan Yin the fire will be quenched. Adrift in an ocean of monsters, if you call on Kuan Yin you will not drown or be eaten. She protects from thunderbolts, goblins, demons, ghosts, giants, wild beasts or poisonous serpents. Call her by name and noxious creatures will vanish.

This great power gave rise to a particular practice. People would live with the *Lotus Sutra*, reading, translating and reciting it constantly. Through this, they would learn to see into past lives, be cured of evil karma, tame demons and cure sickness and possession.

As we have seen, one meaning of the Bodhisattva's name is 'Hearer of the Cries of the Suffering World'. She promises to heed the call of any being who 'cries out on the night'. It is this cry that is our connection to Kuan Yin, for it expresses our wound, the wound of being human. From a moan to a cry of tri-umph or despair, a lonely protest, a demand for justice, a desperate supplication for healing, aloud or uttered in the silence of the heart, these 'calls of the dead' are the garland of her name and rouse her infinite compassion. Lonely, hungry, sick, mourning, crying for meaning, justice, help or understanding, she will be with us. And as the master of 'skillful means' (*upaya*), the range of her powers is impressive. She can break the chain of cause and effect to save us from fire, drowning, shipwreck, murder, demons internal and external, despair, poverty, snakes and insects, legal punishment, falling from mountains or buildings, civil war or greedy warlords. She grants children to longing couples and can manifest instantly in any one of at least thirty-three forms. In her infinite moment of compassion, Kuan Yin hears our cry and becomes our answer. She is the spiritual embodiment of our innate desire for happiness and freedom from suffering.

The Faces of the Goddess

Traditionally, Kuan Yin manifests herself in many ways, each of them reflecting a particular quality of her being. The traditional faces of the Great Compassionate One range from the Water Moon, where she is seen seated on the Western Mountain of Paradise gazing at the reflection of the full moon in the still sea, to a many-headed, many-armed figure of active intervention. There are images for each of her powers of salvation: rescuer from fire, flood or attack; bestower of children; guide of souls to the Pure Land; queen of healing; and 'unfailing rope' of liberation. She stands beside the Diamond Throne of Sakyamuni at Bodh Gaya, the most sacred site in the Buddhist world, to confer the gift of fearlessness in the midst of troubles and terrors. The six syllable Sanskrit mantra OM MANE PADME HUM, which she shares with Avalokitesvara, is recited throughout the East to invoke her. New images are still being born.

One of the earliest, most loved and most known images is the **White Kuan Yin**. The Goddess is seated, cloaked in white, the color of death, purity and completion. She is in a lotus seat, right leg over left, and holds a lotus and a vase. Here she is the Lotus Sutra, pouring out compassion and a flowering of mind that frees us from the murk of the world.

The **Child-giver** or **Willow Branch** Kuan Yin is Queen of Healing. She holds a rosary, suggesting purification of the cycle of birth and death, and a willow branch, symbol of Buddhist virtues. The willow bends and springs back; its weeping is a sign of both compassion and the yielding, powerful force of the woman and the yin. This image is often used in exorcisms and is a tool for spirit mediums. It grants children to couples who long for them.

The **Thousand-Armed and Thousand-Eyed Kuan Yin** is an extraordinary image, coming from a story in which she offered her eyes and her arms to save the misguided father who was persecuting her. Here she is all-embracing and all-seeing, mistress of skillful means, ready to intervene in all situations. Each hand holds a weapon or an implement of rescue, among them the Thunderbolt of Enlightenment and the Ax that Cuts All Attachments and Opens the Bodhi Path.

Kuan Yin of the Southern Ocean, the Star of the Sea, is the protector of sailors, travelers and wayfarers on the Sea of Life. She is seated, calm and smiling, held up by the waves in the middle of a roiling sea full of leaping dolphins and fish. She is master of storms, both literal and emotional. There are temples to this Kuan Yin of the Oceans, protector from shipwreck and drowning, in every seaport in China and India.

The many-handed **Armed Warrior** represents self-purification. She carries a bow, a shield and has a weapon in each of her many hands. In this guise, she combats and destroys the psychological monsters that assail us: demons, ignorance, hungry ghosts, hell-beings and compulsive greed. There are **Three-Headed** and

Eleven-Headed images of Kuan Yin that express protection for the process of spiritual transformation. The **Horse-headed Kuan Yin**, surrounded by dark flames, protects and delivers from a bad rebirth.

In Japan, Kuan Yin became **Kannon**, arriving in the seventh through ninth centuries when pilgrims brought Buddhist texts back from China, first among them her Lotus Sutra. It was translated by the great prince Shotoku (574–622 BCE), who was said to be an incarnation of Kannon. As **Water Moon** and **Virtue King**, this Kannon links the spirit and the natural world. She appears as a nun, a snake, a bird, a dragon or the white Karuna Bird to endlessly combat the evils that beset us. As **Koyasu**, she assures women an easy birth. Kannon is much honored throughout the 'New Buddhist' and 'New Shinto' movements in Japan's religious revivals.

Kuan Yin revealed another of her great powers in Japan, where she presides over dream incubation. Pilgrims harassed by longstanding problems would journey to her shrines and vow to spend a specified time in retreat there, sleeping in the main hall of the temple near the inner sanctuary. Kannon would appear in a dream, often on the last night of the stay, as herself, her miraculous **Boy Servant** or an old **Buddhist Priest**. She cures incurable sickness, consoles inconsolable sorrow and gives dreamers a glimpse of their fate.

In Tibet and India, this figure is the **Rainbow of Tara**. In Hindu thought, she is the *shakti*, power peculiar to all the gods, without which they can do nothing. She is Brahma the Creator's power of flowing words that bring revelation; she is Vishnu the preserver's counterpart, Maya the weaver of the world; and in Shiva the destroyer, she is Gauri, the Radiant White One, the glittering white of the glacier, or Kali, the Black One, with her Necklace of Skulls. Above all she is celebrated as *tarati* or Tara, 'she in the mind who leads out, beyond the darkness of bondage to redemption'.

Tara, like Kuan Yin, is the Great Goddess as a protector and redeemer. She 'happily leads us out' (*Tarati iti Tara*) of dangerous defiles and menacing terrors, crossing the roaring rivers of samsara, delusion and compulsive desire. She protects against water, fire and wind, elephants and snakes, demons, imprisonment, thieves and the power of kings. Like the *Stella Maris* or Star of the Sea, she is 'mistress of boats', served by a flock of boat women who rescue the shipwrecked.

Like Kuan Yin, Tara proclaims: 'I take my worshipers across the ocean of dangers!' She is the *shakti* or power of Avalokitesvara, worshiped as *Prajna Paramita*, mother of all Buddhas and spiritual perfections. As **White Tara**, her emblem is a book resting on a lotus and her hands form the closing of the circle that gives rise to liberation. The Buddhas and Bodhisattvas are her children, casting her light into the world of illusion. As **Green Tara** she is the goddess bestowing benefit on all, while her blue, yellow, red and black forms are her manifestations in the hell worlds, carrying swords and wearing the Necklace of Skulls. The whole sea of life is in her power; she saves those who call to be saved and raises them like lotus blossoms to the surface of the waters, and as Mistress of Desires and Joys she accompanies others in the dark waters below that are full of monsters and glittering with pearls. Each of her sacred pools is a *tirtha*, a ford to cross the waters to the Other Shore and be free of the ego's compulsive greed. The gods themselves 'drink and bathe in the waters of her womb and are freed from the prison of the ego to move to their place in the heavens'.

In all of these forms we see the compassion and mercy of the Bodhisattva, extending help and salvation to all who call on her. For millions, she is a present help in times of danger, a source of grace and beauty who 'sees and hears the cries of the world'. Goddess of the poor, the needy, and the troubled, she is a beacon for all on the storm-tossed seas of this life.

The Tomb World and the Other Shore

In the Pure Land scriptures, religious texts that describe paradise free from compulsion and suffering where reborn souls learn the Great Way and the Nature of Reality, Kuan Yin is connected with the Buddha Amitabha, the Future Buddha who creates the Western Paradise. Kuan Yin guides souls to this paradise, opening gates throughout many realms of existence, from the Hells to the Realms of the Gods. In doing this, she opens a part of each of us that is free from suffering and compulsion and is thus able to experience insight, compassion and great joy.

Meditation scriptures describe a visualization practice that leads to rebirth in Western Paradise and a connection to the Protectors in this life. Kuan Yin or Avalokitesvara is visualized as a golden-skinned being with a great crown of wondrous wish-fulfilling gems, in each of which is a Buddha. Many-colored light streams forth from this Manifestation Body (*nirmanakaya*) to the various realms, becoming Bodhisattvas who accomplish works of compassion. Rays of soft light extend from their hands to assist all the sentient beings.

Kuan Yin as gate to the paradise world or Pure Land exemplifies something seen in almost all religious systems and spiritual practices, the presence of two basic sorts of experience, often seen as landscapes or places. This seems to be something deep in the human experience of the divine.

One world, the one in which we live much of the time, is seen as a Tomb World, characterized by compulsive emotions and mechanical cause and effect. It is a world in which we are the dead. Unconsciously manipulated by images of sex and power, driven by the negative emotions of greed, rage, hatred and ignorance, we lose our ability to see a spiritual dimension to things, never realizing where or what we are. Just as an unclean vessel spoils its contents, the Tomb World poisons the heart and soul of those who give themselves over to it.

In its most radical expression, that of the Gnostics and Manicheans who influenced the development of the Savior-Figure Kuan Yin, this is a world composed of corpses and the excrement of demons, an abyss of evil, a 'self-devouring scab' dissolving and consuming itself. It is an 'empested earth' of smoke, fire, wild winds, fouled waters and dense darknesses, each with its own foul taste. It is full of stupid monsters who revolt and struggle, seeking only to destroy each other. Our feeling of horror and revulsion when we see this world clearly is a sign of both our otherworldly origin and our present enslavement.[3] In modern terms, this is a world of consumerism and desperate greed, articulated by lies and advertising. It is dominated by multinational corporations, the profit motive and sexual compulsion. This greed and lust for power poisons everything it touches, creating a world of 'Every Man for Himself' that turns us each against the other.

Pure Land or paradise, on the other hand, is a clean, bright place full of delight, enclosed and protected from the Tomb World around it.[4] It is a 'Land of the Living' in contrast to the land of the dead, an oasis, island, mountain, garden or jeweled city that is the source of great rivers and the waters of life. Desire is satisfied here, not repressed or exploited. People, animals and spirits understand each other. Killing is not necessary to live.

The experience of the Pure Land or paradise opposes the vicious and deadening state of mind represented by the Tomb World. It is a world outside linear time and space and mechanical cause and effect that offers a variety of imaginative enjoyments and truths. Souls are reborn here wrapped in a lotus which unfolds to show the truth of their eternal nature and the reality of compassion and joy. Pure Land points out the illusory nature of the material building blocks of the Tomb World and releases the experience of freedom, intelligence, beauty and joy. Once in the Pure Land, we will never be dragged back into the Hell Worlds.

This Pure Land captured the imagination of ordinary people throughout the East, giving them a 'lifeline to the spirit' in very bad times indeed when organized religion had become prohibitively complicated. It was associated with several religious practices: visualization of the Bodhisattva, Recitation of her Mantra and, a very important practice indeed, using the Oracle of Kuan Yin in order to open communication with her paradise.

The central characteristic of this paradise, however, seems to be Fullness of Being, a stark contrast to our earthly deprivation and its extremes of wealth and poverty. With a flowing abundance of food, life, communication, creativity, space, beauty, intelligence, freedom and spontaneity, along with the release from greed, lust, ignorance and compulsion, paradise presents desire and fulfillment in a self-renewing circle that we enter through ecstasy and joy. As we put on our Body of Light, we are freed from the deadly battle of the opposites and join the sensual and the spirit together. We are taught the nature of reality by the Healing Teachers and introduced to the Great Images that make the worlds. There are pearls, jewels, golden flowers, trees of fire, joy, song, laughter, music, beautiful maidens and desires fulfilled in paradise. There are no swamps, deserts or poisons. It is a state of continual intoxication that finally satisfies our enormous thirst for meaning.

This paradise world at the 'confluence of two seas' is also seen as a great ark or enclosure where the seeds of all things dwell. It keeps us safe as we cross the Sea of Suffering. Kuan Yin often opens the gates to this paradise in a mountain or sea-grotto from which she listens to the cries of the suffering. These gates were called 'Potulaka Mountain' or 'Potulaka Island' and several people claimed to have literally found them. The monk-traveler Hsuan-tsang (eighth century CE) said they were hidden on the Malay coast. In the tenth century they were discovered on an island off the south China seaport of Ning-po. This particular *P'u-t'o shan* (Potulaka Mountain) is still an important pilgrimage center. In

Japan, the paradise of Kannon was located at the Kumano Shire in the mountains of the Ki peninsula near Nikko and at the Kasuga Shrine in Nara. The Potala Palace in Lhasa, built in the seventeenth century as home of the Dalai Lama, was also thought to be a paradise of Kuan Yin/Avalokitesvara. However, though these and other great shrines certainly carry a numinous power, Kuan Yin's paradise truly opens from what the Chinese called the *hsin* or heart-mind, the uncorrupted 'thought of the heart'. As a famous sage once remarked, 'P'u T'o Island is really in the heart.'

The Savior and the Bridge

But why are we in this situation? Why do religious systems consistently portray us as living in a Tomb World cut off from the experience of paradise? And even more important, what can we do about it? People have been asking these questions ever since the first shamans climbed the World Tree to journey back to the Home of the Gods that was spread out across the night sky. Our situation has been explained as a product of our Own Sin, of a design flaw in creation itself or as the result of a great catastrophe, a flood, fire or collision of planets. It has been described as the nadir of a long cycle or circle, *kaliyuga* or the Iron Age, or as the direct result of the introduction of hierarchical civilization, 'killing Mr Chaos by giving him eyes and ears and a mouth'. But whatever its cause – hubris, original sin, a Bad Time or patriarchal morality – it is the second question that is the more important: what can we do about it? That is the question that the Bodhisattva seeks to answer.

Humans do not suffer just because there are two worlds. We suffer when we confuse the spiritual and the earthly and seek paradise, an innate and totally legitimate human desire, through sex, power and greed. According to many religious disciplines, the solution to our problem is to first separate or discriminate between the worlds and then to link them in a creative and vital way. Unfortunately, we don't seem to be able to do this by ourselves. We must be awakened from our sleep or 'living death' by a force greater than our Greedy Ego. That is the function of the Savior or Redeemer, who acts as a bridge or a boat that sails the troubled waters between the Tomb World and the Pure Lands.

The figure of the Redeemer or Awakened One is one of humanity's most powerful myths or archetypes, and like all archetypes it has a light and a dark side. There have been many demonic saviors in our history, caricatures of the Redeemer running the gamut from the gnostic Demiurge and his Demonic Archons to Hitler or Mao-tse Tung. But our helpers have also been many – Asklepios, Isis, Hercules, Buddha, Jesus, Lao-t'zu, Mani, the Virgin and the Saints, the Daimon and the Guardian Angels.

The Redeemer or Savior asserts the radical presence and reality of the spirit: 'This night you shall be with me in Paradise,' said Christ on the cross to the Thief who hung beside him. The Redeemer shows us that freedom, joy and enlightenment are truly and immediately possible. We can be freed from our chains now, by recognizing both our participation in the paradise world and its radical difference from the world of mortality, greed and mechanical cause and effect. 'Work on your salvation with diligence,' said the Buddha. The Redeemer opens a bridge to the other shore through the eternity of her words and actions. These words and actions are *symbols*, continually re-enacting themselves in violation of the rules of the Tomb World. The Savior, Redeemer or Bodhisattva is a continual *symbolic process*, a bridge to the imaginal world, an experience of the spirit of paradise.

Names and Symbols

'What's in a name?' Juliet asked. 'A rose by any other name would smell as sweet.' She was profoundly wrong, as her tragic destiny shows all too clearly, for it was her name that finally killed both her and the man she loved. Both were trapped by the prison of their names. Romeo was killed by the prison of 'Montague'; Juliet by the prison of 'Capulet'. So let us pay very close attention to naming.

Some very important thinkers have maintained that our fall into the Tomb World came about – and comes about each day – because of our nasty habit of naming things, of assigning them a *sign* that defines their nature and fixes them in a specific place within a hierarchy of meaning. We think that this kind of naming gives us power over things. Adam named the animals so they could not change shape when they wanted to but would come when he called. The Chinese Confucians named everything (*ming*) so they could stop the moving world and turn it into a properly behaved society. Both killed what the Taoists called Mr *Hun-tun*, Old Mr Chaos. We could also call him Mr Paradise.

In this sense a name is a *sign* that *stands in for* a thing; it takes the place of the thing, controls it and cuts us off from the experience of it. The sign is characteristic of the Tomb World. It makes things 'work'. The *symbol*, however, is something else again. It is characteristic of paradise. It connects us to the mystery of a thing. It is a bridge, a gate, a link between worlds. Orders, technical descriptions, scientists, most contemporary schoolrooms, universities, churches and businesses use signs. Poems, dreams, spirits, diviners, real teachers and Bodhisattvas use symbols. Paradise itself is a symbolic reality.

These symbols have variously been called dragon holes, *hsiang*, images, spirits, poems and teachings. The Greeks called them *kairoi*, holes in the web of time and space through which spirit could be 'thrown'. Chinese diviners called them *shi*, eternal 'moments' that link the inner and the outer worlds. Anything we encounter can be 'symbolized' or turned into a symbol, for symbolizing is a way of seeing that gives power to the spirit. This *symbolizing* is one of the great tools of the redeemer, what the Buddhists call *upaya* or 'skillful means'. It helps people understand themselves in a new way and redirects their consciousness. It makes them happier in this world, thus freeing them to exhibit compassion by pointing at the insight or wisdom that reality is symbolic rather than literal. A major use of this symbolizing is in divination, one of the most important skillful means in the Bodhisattva's hands.

Here is an example of 'symbolizing'. Let us imagine that one day long ago someone worrying deeply about the value of what she was doing and who she was went walking in a gentle valley where a stream ran through a grove of bamboo. The wind stirred the leaves. The water softly murmured. She found herself gazing at a stand of supple, hollow bamboo stalks that rose from the welling source of the water. She had a sudden vision that she was like the joints of the bamboo, passing the living water down through the generations, handing it on that all might drink. This spontaneous movement in her imagination became a symbol in Kuan Yin's *Book of Fates*:

• 55 The Eternal Spring

A long row of bamboo stalks
joined together
reaches to a bubbling spring.
Generation after generation can draw on the water.

There is a famous description of this process in *Ta chuan*,[5] the Great Treatise that accompanies China's oldest divination system,

the *I Ching* or *Classic of Change*. There we are told that the ancient
Sage-king Fu Hsi created the fundamental images of the book
through this very process of 'symbolizing' (*hsiang*).

In antiquity Fu Hsi ruled the world we live in.

> *He looked up and saw the figures hanging down from Heaven.*
> *He looked down and saw the patterns on the Earth.*
> *He saw markings on birds and animals*
>   *and the places where they lived on the earth.*
> *He drew on what was near within his body.*
> *He drew on what was far.*
> *He spontaneously symbolized the Images*
>   *to connect us with the bright spirits*
> *and to show us the natures of all the myriad things.*

Symbolizing or *hsiang* makes images that have the power to
connect the visible world of your problems to the invisible world
of the spirit. The images of a divination system are all *hsiang*, created by the kind of imaginative induction we just saw, which is
also called *hsiang*. We use divination to *hsiang* something, to turn
a problem into a symbol, for we *hsiang* things by imagining: we
create images, imitate, act and act out, play, write or divine. In this
way we make a connection between the invisible world of the
spirit and the visible world of our lives.

When we do this, when we see our selves and our lives as
symbolic of spirit, we acquire a special power or virtue, what the
Taoists called *te*. *Te*, which I translate as *power and virtue* or *potency*
or *actualizing-tao*, is a very old word. It is closely associated with
tao, as in the *Tao-te ching* or *Way-Power Classic*. *Te* is the power or
virtue that allows something to fully exist. It is a kind of realizing
power that people and objects acquire that can be accumulated
and nurtured. In the human world, it is the charisma or inner
power that makes a 'great person' (*ta jen*) great. Powerful *te* makes

a powerful person. Exalted *te* makes a wise person or sage. Someone full of *te* is numinous because they have the power to realize the way or *tao* in their own person. By accumulating and refining *te*, we are able to lead our own lives, to be who the spirit means us to be, to participate in paradise. Divination is a way to accumulate *te*. It helps to change our greedy and insecure ego trapped in the Tomb World into a spirit-ego possessing the powerful imagination necessary to connect with the paradise of the symbols.

Divination and the Gift of the Goddess

When we pose a question that expresses a real 'cry from the heart', Kuan Yin will appear to us. This beloved and very powerful spirit directly expresses her great compassion through divination, dreams, magical formulas and mediumistic practices, a very old complex that affirms the bond between the human and the divine in the most immediate terms. From this connection flows the experience we call 'paradise', an 'acquaintance', to use a gnostic term, with the source of reality.

We can see this throughout the world today. People visit shamans, healers and soul doctors, consult oracles, check propitious dates, use sticks, stones, bones and cards to orient themselves with the spirits. They do this not just because they want to know what will happen to them, but because they seek to act in harmony with what the Chinese called the *tao* or Way, the on-going process of the real.[6]

This mixture of fortune-telling, practical guidance and spiritual experience seems strange to us, with our culture's concern for great transcendental truths. It cuts across normal boundaries to join the simple events of everyday life with the experience of the divine. It lets us realize that the events and emotions that sweep through us, our loves and hates, confrontations, problems and long-ings, are the product of spiritual forces with lessons to learn and tolls to pay. Becoming aware of this is a great healing gift, a gift of the Compassionate One.

From this perspective, divination is not just telling the future: it is a *lumen* or light added to our normal intelligence that can give us insight into our fate or inner spirit, locate us in a process of transformation or give us signs of the times that connect us to the flow of the way. The symbols used in this kind of wisdom divina-tion offer themselves as a crossroads, a meeting place with the gods and spirits. Together, they form a navigation system, creating an awareness that mirrors the creative process we call destiny or fate. They open a potent imaginative space where we can interact with the 'helping spirit', our angel or daimon.

If you asked someone in an old culture what divination does, you would probably get a variation on the idea that it gives you access to a divine mind, a world soul or weaver of fates. By using it, you become an object of divine attention and compassion. Divination is a truly aboriginal act, fundamental to religion, magic, myth and the acquaintance with the spirit. No one knows who 'invented' these ways of interacting with fate, or where the symbols come from, but they all point to a kind of fertile chaos deep in the mind where each symbol implicates all other symbols. We do know that opening a dialogue with this fertile chaos is a deeply healing process.

The 100 Poems and the Sticks of Fate

Kuan Yin's main divinatory system is called *Chien Tung* or the *Sticks of Fate*. Like other similar systems, the sticks are the key to her *100 Poems* (four-line images with seven characters in each line) that have different sorts of commentary attached to them.

These *Sticks of Fate* and *100 Poems* are used throughout the world, from Beijing to Hong Kong, from the Sacred Mountains to the urban temples and countryside shrines. You can find them in Taiwan, London, New York, Vancouver, Singapore and San Francisco if you know where to look. They are a defining feature of the diaspora of the Chinese world.

Kuan Yin's *100 Poems* and *Sticks of Fate* are part of a kind of divining that goes back to the great *Chou I* or *I Ching*, the *Classic of Change*[7] that dates from at least 1100 BCE. *I Ching* is the world's greatest wisdom divination system, with roots in the very old practice of the *wu* or mediums, who gave the *shen* or bright spirits a voice in human life. It was the most significant book in traditional China, and each re-interpretation of its use marked a change in the culture. A great commentary literature grew up around its figures, while its words became an integral part of popular culture.

The *I Ching* is made up of sixty-four Figures or Symbols, each made up of a six-line diagram (*gua*) and a series of oracular texts attached to it. These sixty-four Figures are thought to 'encompass' the *tao* or Way, symbolized by the winding river or Dragon's Path. Using it is thought to put you in touch with the helping spirits by opening a 'hole in time' (*shi*), a 'Dragon Hole' that leads you to the Other Shore. It was China's first book, made out of inter-woven bamboo slats that bear a great resemblance to Kuan Yin's sticks. This assemblage defined a special group of diviners known as the 'bamboo shamans' or 'men of the book'.

A leading western psychologist once remarked that whenever you consult an oracle like the *I Ching*, you commit a metaphysical act of great significance.[8] You tune into a process that connects individual and universal fate and confirms you as a meaningful part of the universe. This is a testimony to your significance, a token of your place in the universe and an expression of care and concern.

In Kuan Yin's oracle this care and concern is directly described in terms of the Bodhisattva Vow. Mahayana Bodhisattvas vow to postpone liberation and remain in the world, exercising compassionate care 'for the happiness of all sentient beings'. These Enlightened Ones or Protectors accumulate vast funds of spiritual merit that they can freely transfer to others (*parinamana*) in order to release them from the suffering of compulsive emotion and aid in their salvation. A major means of effecting this transfer is the practice of divination.

> The Moon rising on the indigo sea,
> A pearl like a seed.
> Open your heart to compassion and change:
> The Protector will blossom there.

You work with Kuan Yin's oracle through a specific process. You pose a question that is based on a knot or tangle in which you are caught. By opening your heart to the answer, you let yourself be 're-arranged' by the symbol or figure (*hsiang*) Kuan Yin gives you. You then act on and act out the symbolic insight you acquire.

In this process, three things are said to happen. Because Kuan Yin, who sponsors the oracle, is a Bodhisattva with unlimited spiritual merit acquired in countless lives led 'for the happiness of all sentient beings', she can freely transfer or 'download' spiritual merit to us through the gate of the symbols. This is the source of the energy and joy that often comes from a divinatory session. She can also take on or 'upload' our entanglements, releasing us from these knots through her enlightened awareness. Her 'reality therapy' breaks the karmic chain of cause and effect and frees us from the compulsion that got us into our tangle in the first place. We 'see' what is going on and acquire the power to navigate through it. This exchange opens the gate to the Pure Land or Western Paradise. It makes each person who uses it feel precious and unique, the focus of the world of the spirit.

Transforming Thirst

The poets, thinkers and diviners who helped to create the oracle of Kuan Yin thought of our soul not as a thing but as a process. Though they believed in 'reincarnation', they did not think that the soul 'enters' a new body, but that it creates a form suitable to its 'thirst' (*trishna*).[9] This thirst is the root of reincarnation and the workings of karma, for trishna brings things into existence. If it wants to see, we have eyes. If it wants to hear, we have ears. If it wants to run we have legs and there are deer and rabbits in the woods; if it wants to fly, we have birds in the sky; if it wants to swim, we have fish in the sea.

This thirst connects us with things. We look at the flower or the bird and appreciate them because something in us participates in their trishna. Trishna is not *in* our consciousness. We are in *it*; it is the inexhaustible ground of our being.

As long as we are human beings, we can never do away with trishna or we would do away with ourselves. Greater Vehicle Buddhists realized this and made it the center of their teaching. The Bodhisattva Vow, the Transfer of Merit and the Oracle of Kuan Yin grow out of it. A Master was once asked, 'How can we rid ourselves of trishna?' He replied quite simply: 'Why should we try?'

But the question is not without meaning, for we suffer from our thirst. By themselves, sentient beings including humans are helpless in the face of trishna. We are bound by the karma of past experience, conditioned by time, space and causality. The more we try to know paradise the deeper we get ourselves into a tangled mess. Help must come from a source outside ourselves that understands our limitations and our suffering. It must be both within us and outside our karmic mess. This is the Bodhisattva and her Vow. Her message is simple.

Trishna, which is needed for the welfare of the entire world, works wrongly only when it associates with the wrong things, when it relies on the greedy ego and its ambitions as the only principle of life. When it is freed from these narrow attachments, it becomes the all-knowing and all-loving Compassionate One herself.

> *I am a happy man indeed!*
> *I visit the Pure Land as often as I like.*
> *There and back,*
> *There and back,*
> *There and back,*
> *Glory to the Compassionate One!*

This poem of Saichi to the Amida Buddha expresses what happens when you enter into dialogue with the Bodhisattva through her divinatory symbols. It sets up a 'frame of faith' that turns you towards the Pure Land and its Goddess and turns her toward you. It 'provides you with all spiritual merit' through her vow of Transfer of Merit and 'cleanses you of the evil passions of former lives' by enrolling you in the 'order of the steadfast'. This does not destroy trishna, it *redirects* it. It turns trishna onto itself through 'knowledge of the transcendental' which is beyond simple greed and causality. Then trishna will work its own way out. It leads directly to *mahakaruna*, the Great Compassion of the Bodhisattva.

This spontaneous process of detachment and transformation is facilitated by using Kuan Yin's divinatory symbols. They connect you with the principle of compassion so that you no longer see yourself as a passive victim of karmic causation. Through this profound change in awareness, you become the 'tent-maker' of fate, the *gahakaraka* itself.

The Necessary Goddess

Kuan Yin is also a Dragon Lady. She reflects a belief in animal gods that is much older than her existence as a Bodhisattva. These animal powers are still with us in dreams and visions as representatives of the sources of life. They speak with gigantic voices, the movers of the world.

Among all these sacred animals – bears, tigers, deer, foxes, horses, sheep, pigs, owls, fishes, tortoises and snakes – the greatest are two that stand in a special relationship to the first two Figures of the *Classic of Change*: the Dragon manifests as *Ch'ien* Force and the Mare manifests in *K'un* Field.[10]

In the old culture, the activity of Heaven was symbolized by the rise of the Dragon from the watery depths to the cloud heavens. The ideogram for *Force* is the dragon's name. It shows the sun's warmth and the shimmering vapors it causes to rise from the earth. This mighty spirit, 'mightiest of the three hundred and sixty scale-bearing animals', both creates and destroys. Dragons call forth the great summer storms that bring rain to fertilize the fields as well as typhoons, earthquakes and floods that devastate the people. As in the six-line figure *ch'ien*, the dragon, at first hidden in the winter waters below the earth, mounts through the fields to the heavens to bring summer rain and thunder. As autumn begins, he returns again to the watery depths.

The Dragon's watery dwelling place is called the Pool of the Thunder (*Lei Tse*), described in the Mountain Sea Classic (*Shan-hai ching*) and the *Huai-nan t'zu*, the Taoist 'encyclopedia'. The thunder god in this pool has the body of a Dragon and a human face. When he beats his belly there is both thunder and laughter (*hsi*: lightning, gleaming; happy, burst into laughter). For Chinese, beating your belly is a sign of the primitive joy of life. The Taoist classic *Chuang-tz'u* (chapter nine) links it with the golden age and paradise:

In the days of the good old ruler Ho-hsü, people stayed home and did not know what to do. When they went out, they didn't know where they should go. When their mouths were full they beamed with joy, beat their bellies (*hsi*) and went walking. This was all the people knew how to do. But then came those Confucian Culture Heroes who made their 'rites and music' to regulate the shape of the world and afflict the people with 'humaneness' and 'duty'. The people began to run around and stumble over each other searching for 'knowledge' and fight with one another in their greed for gain. Soon there was no rest and no happiness. All this was the fault of those Heroes.

Just as the people of that blessed old time before Confucian knowledge and greed took over, the Thunder Dragon beats his belly and laughs. He lifts his huge, glistening greeny-blue body from the pool, exposing his white underside, and thumps his belly so that the mountains ring. Terrible Dragon laughter spurts from his mouth like lightning. The storms lash the lake and the rain drives on in furrows, fecundating, blessing and flooding. This laughing, creative, frightening joy is the Dragon. His grinning face can break through the mask of the ordinary at any moment.

Like Kuan Yin, Dragons (*lung*) live in both the waters and the heavens. They rise from the deep, from springs and wells, rivers and swamps, lakes and oceans. They guard the treasures of the sea and hold up the dwellings of the gods.

It is the treasure-guarding dragons that gave Kuan Yin her Great Pearl. If you look up at the central panel in a Chinese temple, you will often see a dragon playing with a silvery pearl, the Pearl of Wisdom and Power, the Treasure Hard to Attain. It is the luminous force within us that unites the upper and lower worlds, fulfills our desires and creates the 'deathless body'. The essence of yin and yang are condensed in the pearl, turned to

sexual energy and vital force and enveloped in the fire of transformation. Truly a 'pearl of great price'.

The Dragon guards and can bestow the pearl stored in his
underwater paradise. Moved by her compassionate rescue of his
son, the Dragon Lord gave this Light that Shines in the Darkness
to Kuan Yin along with his daughter Lung Nü, the Dragon
Maiden. This pearl lets Kuan Yin open the gates to the Pure Land
as she sits in a grotto deep in meditation, flanked by the Dragon
Girl and the Golden Boy, while the waves surge and play around
her. The pearl she confers fulfills all desires and gives us entrance
to paradise.

Kuan Yin, however, does not enter the Pure Land. She has
vowed never to rest until every being is released from suffering.
Through this vow, she becomes the second great animal, counterpart of the Dragon, the Mare (*pin ma*) roaming the wide fields
of the earth. The Mare is the animal spirit of the second great
Figure of the *Classic of Change*, *K'un* or Field. She is the Necessary
Goddess.

For those who consult the oracle and obtain its help and power,
Ch'ien or Force 'supplies security and brings things to a good
end' through the Dragon. The second Figure, *K'un* or Field, 'supplies security and brings things to a good end through the Mare'.
Kuan Yin has the treasure of the Dragon; but she works in the sign
of the Mare.

The oldest form of the Mare is the great Mother Goddess. She
reaches far back into prehistory, to a time before the origins of the
Change when people could talk directly with spirits. If you ride
this power, you are 'easily and safely carried to the goal'. The text
of this Figure says that profit and insight come from 'following,
not leading'. The Earth acts for Heaven to assure humans a 'quiet
supply of security' and will 'open the way or *tao*'.

The phrase 'supplies security and brings things to a good
end' translates a single Chinese oracular character: *chen*, or trial.[11]

Its meanings include: an inquiry by divination and the result, to be righteous and firm, to separate the wheat from the chaff. It represents the enduring kernel or core of things. The ideogram contains the graph for divination and the graph for pearl: divination is the way to obtain Kuan Yin's pearl and the security and benefit of the tireless Mare.

Change says that the mare 'roams the earth without bound', giving and 'supplying security'. An age-old tradition underlies this figure, the tradition of the 'dark animal goddess' or Valley Spirit seen in *Lao-t'zu*:

> *The Valley Spirit never dies.*
> *It is named Dark Animal Goddess.*
> *The door of the Dark Animal Goddess*
> *Is called the Root of Heaven and Earth.*
> *Like an endless thread she endures.*
> *You can call upon her easily.*

This Goddess carries an ancient heritage of divinatory proverbs. She is called Mother of Heaven and Earth, a term applied only to the *tao* or way itself. The 'Mother of the World' (*t'ien-hsia mu*), who is 'so quiet and so empty', acts through the 'images and seeds' of the divinatory signs to give home and refuge to all creatures. Kuan Yin as Mare is the Way of the Mother, the Necessary Goddess bringing the 'pearl' to all creatures. She is the 'divine, clairvoyant something of the Woman's Way'.

> *He who has found this mother*
> *Understands he is a child.*
> *When he understands he is her child*
> *And clings to her*
> *He will be without danger when the body dies.*

> *Use the small and see clearly.*
> *Be flexible to be strong.*
> *Use this light to return to clarity.*
> *You will lose nothing when you die.*
> *It is called putting on what lasts forever.*

In the figure of Kuan Yin, the Necessary Goddess was restored to the place from which she was banished by Confucian Saints and Spiritual Patriarchs. She is, even today, a new recognition of the eternal power and compassion of the Mare and the Way.

The Melting Pot

The literal history of Kuan Yin begins with the coming of Buddhism to China. Her qualities are first described in the Chinese translation of the *Lotus Sutra*, a sermon by the Buddha Sakyamuni given from the Mount of Vultures. It was written down in the first century CE and translated into Chinese about 400 CE. In this sutra we are told that the Bodhisattva can appear in any world, in any form from god or goddess to monk, prostitute or demon. The figure is described as wisdom's sun, subduer of woes, illuminator of the world, divine thunder and spiritual rain that quenches distress, desire and pain.

Originally androgynous or male, by 800 CE Kuan Yin emerged in female form. This transformation occurred in the great religious melting pot of China's rugged Northwest, at the head of the Silk Road leading to the Middle East and Mediterranean Europe. From here, the cult of Kuan Yin spread throughout China and into Korea and Japan in the ninth and tenth centuries, linking with and transforming other goddesses – the Old Mountain Mother, the Azure Cloud Mother, the Great Mother of the West, the Sea-Goddesses of China's many port cities, the tribal and mountain Mothers who protect birth and children and the Dark Female, the Valley Spirit of the Taoists. She carried with her the peculiar kind of 'shamanism' and divination practiced by the *wu* or spirit mediums so vigorously attacked by orthodox Confucians. If the arrival of the Lotus Sutra was the door through which she entered China, in a way she was already there. Her 'feminine' oracular practice is the ground of her widespread popular success and the deep love people have for her: she answers individuals in distress, and ordinary people face hell every day. They flock to the solace and insight she offers.

Lightning Flashes in the Dark of Night

The Northwest in 600–800 CE was a great religious melting pot where Mayahana or Tantric Buddhists mixed with Mandeans and Manicheans and Nestorians, Zoroastrians, Sufis, Taoists and practicing spirit-mediums. All were outlaws in one way or another, proscribed by various orthodoxies from Christian to Confucian, and they lived in the dangerous and treacherous world of the Silk Road, with its robber bands and vast desert stretches. All of these 'outlaw' religions seemed to believe in two things: a radical separation between the endless wheel of birth, death, greed and suffering and a fertile spiritual world that the individual could reach. Religion was a vital need, the need for a connecting link between these worlds that could save them from being abandoned to an eternal hell. The world had reached a point where enlightenment could no longer be achieved by traditional means, which had become elitist, over-complicated and stale. From this crisis of faith came the living image of the Redeemer and Protector, the flash of lightning in the dark of night. The starting point for the emergence of this figure was the Mahayana re-imagining of the Bodhisattva Vow.[12]

May I be a guard for those who are protectorless,
A guide for those who journey on the road;
For those who wish to go across the water,
May I be a boat, a raft, a bridge.

May I be an isle for those who yearn for landfall,
And a lamp for those who long for light;
For those who need a resting place, a bed;
For those who need a servant, may I be a slave.

May I be the wishing jewel, the vase of plenty,
A word of power, and the supreme remedy.
May I be the trees of miracles,
And for every being, the abundant cow.

Like the great earth and the other elements,
Enduring as the sky itself endures,
For the boundless multitude of living beings,
May I be the ground and vessel of each life.

Thus for every single thing that lives,
In number like the boundless reaches of the sky,
May I be their sustenance and nourishment
Until they pass beyond the bounds of suffering.

Teachers, Buddhas, Bodhisattvas, listen!
Just as you, who in the past have gone to bliss,
Conceived the awakened attitude of mind,
Likewise for the benefit of beings
I will generate the same attitude.

May I attain Buddhahood!
May I attain Buddhahood!
May I attain Buddhahood!

Part of the Answer or Part of the Problem

The second element in this religious melting pot was Gnostic. Between 400–600 CE, various sects associated with the 'great heresy' of Gnosticism entered Northwest China, driven out of the Mediterranean area by the violent persecution of the Orthodox Church. Gnostics were not really heretic Christians; they were pseudo-Christian just as they were pseudo-Jewish and pseudo-Pagan. They represented an ancient strain of thought that attached itself to various symbol systems and 'deconstructed' them in order to orient us toward the *gnosis* or direct 'acquaintance with the spirit', a practice that may have originated in an old, pre-Rabbinic form of Jewish worship. This Gnostic stream flows through Manichean and Mandean thought into the great melting pot of Northwest China, the beginning and end of the Silk Road.

Gnostics saw the passions as demons that literally fasten onto our soul like wolves on a kill and turn us toward compulsive materialism. The Gnostic figure of Sophia the Redeemer who reaches out to awaken the divine spark in each being may have been the catalyst that produced Kuan Yin, the Compassionate One, out of her male form, Avalokitesvara.

Gnostics saw three kinds of people in the world with three kinds of souls: the *pneumatikoi* or spirit-people who were saved because their souls were open to the voice of the redeemer; the *psychoi* or soul-people who, though dense and more literal-minded, could be saved through hard work and good deeds; and the *hylikoi* or greed-people who were consumed with negative emotions and given over to the demons. Put imaginatively, their question becomes a very important one: which soul am I acting out of? Which perspective governs my experience of reality? Am I part of the Answer or part of the Problem?

Don't Try to Help Heaven!

Once born, Kuan Yin was clothed in the mystery of the *tao*, the Taoist valley spirit or 'on–going process of the real' that nourishes all the myriad beings. If Confucianism is the harsh, stern father of the Chinese world, Taoism is its accepting and yielding mother. Its mood is joyful and irreverent. It is open to the occult and meta-physical side of experience that Confucians keep at a distance. Taoist ritual permeates popular culture, part of a religious tradition that includes trance, spirit mediums and spirit journeys, alchemy, exorcism and psychic transformation.

The philosophical side of Taoism rests on two books, the *Lao-tz'u* or *Tao Te Ching* and the *Chuang-tz'u*.[13] Each contains deliberate and often hilarious attacks on orthodox Confucian morality and heroic egotism. Taoism is a spiritual affirmation of chaos, spontaneous creativity and the central importance of 'doing nothing' (*wu-wei*).

The *Lao-tz'u* or *Tao Te Ching* began as a book for rulers. It suggested that a ruler can rule through *tao* rather than violence and exploitation. When the ruler loves quietude and acts by not-acting (*wu-wei*), the people will spontaneously follow the straight path and prosper. He does not disturb their peace with analysis, give speeches about virtue or stir up ambition. He knows that when you use intellect, the great lies begin; when you disturb families, 'dutiful sons' arise; when you have confused everything with silly plans, 'loyal subjects' appear. All these things have no *tao* whatsoever.

Taoism condemned the ideals of conventional Confucian morality – its virtue, its laws, its love of ritual and its hierarchical view of the family. Most of all it despised the act of giving things names (*ming*) that subsume the individual in an abstract category. By naming what we desire and taking the name for the reality, we split the opposites and call up our nemesis. By striving to 'do good', we bring evil into the world.

So what can we do? According to Taoists, the way to act in the world is to voluntarily assume the 'woman's role'. There are many images for this: flowing water, the uncarved block, child, female, mother, valley spirit, dark door, empty vessel, for it is the womb of creation. We can open this space within ourselves and return to the source of all things. *Tao*, the mysterious highest good, then manifests itself in our spontaneous, non-aggressive compassionate behavior.

Chuang-tz'u is the first text in Chinese history to present a way of wisdom for the individual in private life. Every educated Confucian gentleman in early China wanted to become the counselor to a Prince, but the *Chuang-tz'u* depicts these would-be politicians as well-fed, decorated oxen being led to slaughter while the author, a happy piglet or an old turtle, blissfully plays in the mud. Everything in the *Chuang tz'u* is designed to insist on the relativity of conventional values and to help its readers dis-identify with conventional ideas. It is the first appearance of a special kind of spiritualized being, the *hsien* or Immortals, who have so freed themselves from mundane collective existence that they have left the turbulent world. Their effortless lives, freedom of movement, natural spontaneity and unpredictability became an image of the Taoist self.

The basic principle of this Taoist education is emptiness. We create a void or empty space in our heart by freeing ourselves from compulsive naming, greedy passions and collective values. Things begin to happen of their own accord without the intervention of the busy ego.

Return is another basic principle of this teaching. Return is the movement of the Way. Let everything return to its starting point. Because we have become empty within, we can return to the source and wander freely, watching the coming and going of the Myriad Beings. We can return to the time before the cosmos was created and history began. We watch the *tao* shaping the universe out of chaos, while yin and yang continually transform it. When we grasp this process, our whole identity becomes fluid. We become like a spirit, a *shen*.[14]

The central practice in this process is *wu-wei*, not-acting. It is an idea, a meditation technique and a way of being in the world. Not-acting is not inaction. We never act, but there is nothing left undone. We stop acting through our ego and greedy personal will and begin acting through the spirit and the *tao*. Taoists feel there is no true achievement without this practice. Using force will sooner or later turn anything you do into the opposite of what you intend. Disaster and failure await.

Here is a famous text from the *Tao Te Ching* that we can imagine a Taoist wanderer proclaiming with glee to a Confucian moralist:

When the tao is lost, then your so-called virtue arises.
When virtue is lost, then your so-called benevolence
    arises.
When benevolence is lost, then your so-called righteous-
    ness arises.
When righteousness is lost, then your so-called doctrine of
    propriety (*li*) arises.
Now this propriety of yours
    is nothing but the empty husk of loyalty and faithfulness.
It is the beginning of all confusion and doubt.

The word 'propriety' (*li*) is a key Confucian term of highest value, so this equation of *li* with the loss of the way diatribe undermines the meanings of all Confucian texts. Taoists realized that when you create an ideal, you must split off its opposite, which falls into the unconscious and becomes a center of attraction, necessitating a constant heroic effort to maintain the repression. Internalizing ideals of Virtue and Propriety involves us in the endless repression of their opposites, both undesirable psychic contents and the people on whom they are projected.

The Friendship of the Spirits

The conflict between Taoist and Confucian really revolves around the meaning of the word *shen*, a term that means both 'spirit' and 'spirits'. *Shen* is basic to the Taoist understanding of the nature and destiny of human beings. It can be realized or actualized and, when it is actualized, it frees you from the endless round of the Tomb World. While Confucians say that *shen* is merely a quality of mind, with nothing immortal about it, Taoists believe it is the key to personal transformation.

Connected with spirit-mediums and shamans, the experience of *shen* comes long before theories of yin and yang or the kinds of soul that correspond to them, the *po* and the *hun*. It is used in the combination *kuei-shen*, ghosts and spirits. It is also used to describe a very special kind of person who is totally realized and thus has become like a spirit, a *shen-jen* or Godlike Person. Confucians kept these realms rigidly separated: 'Revere the spirits and keep them at a distance' was Confucius' view of *shen*. Taoists cultivated those moments when we cross the line into spirit. They found them inspiring, liberating and true to the facts of the soul.

The word *shen* was also used to describe a very particular transformation in religious thought and practice that occurred about 400 BCE. Taoists transformed the meaning of the word by adding the meaning 'spirits in here', spirits who lived in our souls, to the traditional meaning 'spirits out there'. They refashioned ancient rituals designed to invite the spirits to come to the altar in a temple by turning them into an invitation to the spirits to dwell in our hearts and souls. The ancient rites of calling the god became the drama of inviting the spirit to become the ruler of your body.[15]

By doing this Taoists gave us an intensely individual experience of spiritual transformation that cut across the distinction between the priest, the medium and the shaman. When the orderly world of Confucian morality collapsed, as it did several times in the history of China, this sense of recovering the indwelling spirits, of 'washing your mind at the gates of mystery', became very important. In *Ta chuan*, the Great Treatise that accompanies the *Classic of Change*, this transformation was used to re-vision the role of divinatory practices. The new idea of the human heart-mind (*hsin*) was expressed in terms such as the 'sanctuary or altar of the spirit' (*ling-fu, ling-t'ai*) or the 'heart-mind of the spirit altar' (*ling-t'ai-hsin*). The Sixth Zen Patriarch called it the 'bright mirror high on the altar wall' (*ming chien tsa kao-t'ai*), found by sweeping away the 'mind of the moment' or greedy-ego mind (*nien*) in a technique called *wu-nien* or no-thought.

> The body like the bodhi tree
> The heart-mind like the altar's
> Bright mirror.

This process of transformation gives you access to a 'bright spirit' that protects you while encouraging you to act out of the best parts of your nature, your deep self. It is a personal way to the spirit, a way of transformation allied to practices of mediumship and spirit possession[16] used by the early spirit-mediums, the women and men who were *wu*. It enables you to 'see and hear what is occulted' and to 'give to those above' (*shen*, the light spirits) 'and those below' (*kuei*, the dark ghosts) 'what is due to them'. This generous power of discrimination causes a luminous spirit (*shen ming* or bright spirit) to take up its home within. You become 'daimonic and clear-seeing', profoundly connected to the invisible world. Here is a statement from the *Kuan tz'u*[17], perhaps the earliest existing Taoist text, that gives a sense of this practice:

Look, there is a *shen* (spirit) within your person.
Now it goes, now it comes.
No one can imagine it . . .

But if you reverently clean its abode
It will return of itself.
You will recover your own true nature,
Fixed in you once for all.

We call on the *shen*, the bright spirit, to take a place in our heart. And as we go on with the work, day by day, suddenly the spirit will arrive.

Born from this great spiritual melting pot, partaking of its many traditions, Kuan Yin, the One Who Sees and Hears the Cries of the World, walked forth among the beings she vowed to cherish and enlighten, breaking all sectarian boundaries. She is equally at home with Buddhists, Taoists, Pagans and Gnostics. The stories of her miracles of healing, deliverance and enlightenment have proliferated in East and West. Her compassion and wisdom offer an exit from the compulsive worlds of greed, lust and power and a return to the true thought of the heart.

Miracles, Stories and Shrines[18]

The Buddhist Caves at Lung Men, near Loyang in Henan Province, and at Tun Huang, at the head of the Silk Road in the rugged Northwest, were perhaps the first sites of the worship of Kuan Yin. From about 650–850 CE, statues, icons and accounts of the miracles of Kuan Yin proliferated in these caves, signaling the rise of a compassionate Buddhism dedicated to salvation for all. It was here that Kuan Yin took on her female appearance and was associated with the Pure Lands and Paradise. Many different Buddhist schools practiced here and joined in worshiping the Compassionate One. Common people flocked to the sites, where the Gates of Paradise were opened. For it was deeply felt that you could no longer attain enlightenment by relying on your own powers. As the Iron Age grew darker and darker, only the infinite compassion of the Bodhisattva could help.

In 939 CE, a magical statue of Kuan Yin was sculpted from a numinous piece of wood washed up near a monastery outside of Hangchow. The dreams of those who found the wood and made the statue said that this was the birth of a Kuan Yin who would protect the entire city. Miracle books and images spread out from Hangchow, including an 'aristocratic' version of her *100 Poems*. A great temple was built and annual fairs and rituals were inaugurated.

Hangchow became both a great pilgrimage site and a leisure resort for China's literati.

The Buddhist Monastery at Hsiang Shan, which housed a famous statue of Ta Pei, a male version of the Thousand-Armed Kuan Yin that had miraculous powers, became another major center of worship when Chiang Chih Ch'i, an important young magistrate, visited the monastery about 1100 CE. The Abbot Huai Chou showed the magistrate a strange manuscript left by a visiting monk that purported to be the Life of the Bodhisattva of Hsiang Shan, the Goddess of Compassion. Chiang thought he had discovered the site of Kuan Yin's last human incarnation and, what is more, that Kuan Yin herself had brought him to the monastery so that he could make her story known. The mysterious manuscript contained a prophecy that three hundred years after it was published the worship of Kuan Yin would blossom like a hundred flowers.

Whatever the real source of the manuscript, Chiang had it inscribed on stone pillars erected in the courtyard, then reproduced and distributed it throughout the land. The poor crumbling monastery was transformed overnight into a spiritual theme park and pilgrimage site for Kuan Yin devotees that lasted over five hundred years!

P'u T'o Island, about seventy miles away from the port of Ningpo, rises abruptly from the South China Sea. Immensely beautiful, it has been a Taoist Magic Mountain refuge for two thousand years. About 800 CE, it was found to be an earthly root of the Paradise Kuan Yin inhabits, the *Potulaka* or mystical paradise described in the Flower Ornament Sutra (*Buddhavatamsaka Sutra* or *Hua yen ching*). In his scripture, a young pilgrim named Sudhana is told by Manjushri, Bodhisattva of Wisdom, to seek out his true friends. His twenty-eighth encounter brought him to Kuan Yin on Potulaka Island.

Paradise Island became an immensely popular pilgrimage site.

Kuan Yin is enshrined at Buddha Peak Monastery, an ancient Taoist sacred site, where her statue is reflected in a huge fishpond below the terraced buildings. There have been numerous sightings and miracles at the Cave of the Tidal Sound, a stunningly beautiful cove with sheer walls. Many, too, have committed suicide or mutilated themselves here in order to break the chain of karma by dying in the Goddess's arms. Today, sadly, it is full of bars, prostitutes and tourists.

The myths and stories of Kuan Yin show her calming, soothing and freeing the myriad beings from the afflictions of greed and poverty, lust and rage. A modern story tells how Kuan Yin solved the Problem of Being in Two Places at Once. Soon after the Ten Thousand Creatures came into being, Kuan Yin was given the task of showing them the Way. At first, all went well. The animals and winged creatures were happy and got on well together.

However, as soon Kuan Yin was called back to the Heavenly Mansions, rage, greed and murder broke out on earth. Kuan Yin heard the cries of the victims and came running back. She settled things once more. But as soon as she left, the carnage started again. This happened several times, until she called a great assembly of all the creatures and demanded to know just why they began to eat each other the moment her back was turned.

'It's all very fine when you are with us,' said the rabbit. 'We aren't afraid, so there is no greed and no fighting and no eating each other up. But when you go we are terrified and it all starts up again.' Kuan Yin thought for a moment, then gestured at a humble gray bird standing near her. Suddenly it was changed into a gorgeous peacock with a hundred eyes in its tail, like the hundred Poems of her oracle. 'These eyes will watch and help you,' she said, 'so I will always be by your side.'

The story in the mysterious manuscript of Hsiang Shan tells of Kuan Yin's Last Human Incarnation as Miao Shan. The story begins when a treacherous usurper named Miao Chung seized power in Hsing Lin, the kingdom in which the monastery was located. This usurper was the father of Miao Shan, who was to become Kuan Yin, the Compassionate One. Denied a son because of his bloody hands, he and his wife had three daughters. Miao Shan was the youngest, and portents such as earthquakes and a miraculous aroma surrounded her birth. She was extremely beautiful and emerged from the womb covered in heavenly clouds.

Miao Shan's parents wanted to marry all their daughters to powerful warlords. Miao Shan, who had grown into a simple, devout and loving girl, refused this marriage. She wished only to become a nun, renouncing the world of greed and treachery. She would only reconsider, she said, if her father could show her how her marriage would heal the three great troubles of the world: old age, illness and death. 'My only desire is to heal the world,' she said. 'I want to heal winter's cold and summer's heat, lust, old age and sickness. I want to make all people equal, rich or poor, and share out all the goods of the world.'

Needless to say, her father was outraged. He made her a palace slave, and her tribulations began. Seeing that she wasn't discouraged by drudgery and insults, he finally sent her off to Hsiang Shan, but insisted she be given the worst possible work to cure her of her fantasies of becoming a nun. Huang Ti, the Lord on High, saw this. He commanded the North Star to send five Mountain Spirits, eight Dragon Ministers and the local Earth Deities to help her. The Sea Dragon dug her a well, tigers brought in firewood, birds collected vegetables and earth gods slaved in the kitchens.

Further enraged on hearing of this, her father sent five thousand hand-picked warriors to burn the nunnery and slaughter the nuns. As the flames broke out, Miao Shan called on Buddha, pricked the roof of her mouth and spat the blood on the flames. The drops of blood became rain clouds that quenched the fire. The troops retreated but were ordered by the evil king to capture Miao Shan and take her to the execution grounds to be killed the next morning.

Huang Ti ordered the Earth God to intervene. When Miao Shan was bound and kneeled before the block, a brilliant light surrounded her. The executioner drew his sword only to see it shatter. He finally had to strangle the poor girl. The Earth God whisked her body away to the forest nearby, gave her a pill of immortality and revived her soul.

Miao Shan then traveled through the Eighteen Hells, each Hell brimming with souls in torment. Her compassion for those who suffered transformed each hell into a paradise, thus ensuring each soul of salvation. The Kings of Hell complained bitterly. She was released from the Hell Worlds, returned to her body where she was given another pill of immortality and spent nine years at Hsiang Shan monastery perfecting her virtues. During that time she asked Buddha for two companions, a miraculous boy and a virtuous girl.

The young man was Shan Ts'ai, a monk released from his body to become her follower, who became the Golden Boy. The virtuous girl was Lung Nü, daughter of the Third Dragon Lord. Miao Shan, now become Kuan Yin, saved his son, when, in the shape of an enormous carp, he was trapped in a fisherman's net. As reward for her compassion, the Dragon Lord gave her the Great Pearl of the Sea, a luminous gem the size and shape of the full moon as reflected in the water. Lung Nü brought the pearl to the Goddess and was so taken by her compassion that she stayed with her forever.

Meanwhile, her father the king had fallen ill. His accumulated evil actions burst forth as a burning fever and running sores all over his body. He was in constant torment, and could neither sleep nor rest. A monk told him that he could only be cured through a medicine made of 'the arm and the eye of one who is without anger'. Such a one dwelt at Hsiang Shan monastery. A messenger was sent immediately.

Kuan Yin confronted this messenger and sternly rebuked the king's evil acts. Then she gouged out her eyes, cut off her arms and bade the messenger to take them to the king. He was healed, for her radical compassion broke the chain of rage by which he was bound.

When the king and queen came to the monastery to give thanks, they were confronted with their mutilated daughter and completely broke down. They begged forgiveness, which Kuan Yin willingly granted. 'Now,' she said, ' I have diamond eyes and golden arms,' revealing herself as the Thousand-Armed and Thousand-Eyed Goddess. The mountain trembled, the sky was filled with many-colored clouds and an indescribably beautiful aroma permeated the air. She ascended into the clouds like the harvest moon, the radiant Bodhisattva. Her parents burned her earthly body, became good Buddhists and ruled well for many years.

As the Star of the Sea, Kuan Yin is surrounded by tales of rescue and deliverance from great danger. Her greatest shrine is on P'u T'o Island, seventy miles offshore from Ningpo, which lies on the major trade routes to Japan and Korea. She has assimilated all the local sea-goddesses, such as A-Ma, protector of Macau, and her shrines overflow with votive ships and anchors, signs of gratitude and love. She can change the course of rivers and seas as well as tame the turbulent flow of fate and desire. The story of The Parting of the Waters at the Bridge of Fu Kien shows her working her miracles with what is at hand.

Fu Kien is on the Lo Yang River, one of the most violent and turbulent rivers in China. For all its violence, it is a busy, vital trade route, with barges full of foodstuffs coming downstream and ships laden with merchandise sailing or being pulled up-river. Many died on the river, but it could never be bridged.

This story begins with a great storm, a typhoon that raised huge waves that threatend to swamp all the ships on the river and drown all the passengers in the turbulent waters. One woman on a small boat in extreme danger called out to Kuan Yin. The woman was pregnant at the time of the disaster. The White Kuan Yin appeared and instantly calmed the storm. The winds died and the clouds dispersed. She said to the frightened young woman who had called on her: 'Have no fear! Your son will live to bridge this river.'

Her son was a diligent, kind and very intelligent boy. He made his way up through the ranks of the examinations and, in time, became First Minister to the Emperor himself. But he never forgot his destiny. He wanted to go back to build the bridge his destiny called on him to build, but the Emperor would not let him go.

One day as he was meditating on this problem in the garden, watching the busy ants stream over a leaf, an idea came to him. He went into the Imperial Garden and drew several characters on a large leaf with honey. The ants were soon attracted and ate their way through the leaf where he had placed the honey. When the Emperor strolled by, he was astounded. He read out the message aloud: 'Ts'ai Hsing, return home at once to fulfill your duty!' Because every one of the Emperor's words is law, Ts'ai Hsing was soon on his way.

At first the work went well, but soon Ts'ai Hsing was stymied. He had to have the river held back in order to sink the foundations for the great pillars that would support the bridge. So he wrote a letter to the Dragon Lord who ruled the river. A humble workman carried it to his underwater palace. Wonderfully, the Dragon King gave his assent – but only for *three days*! The work must be done in *three days*! On the appointed day, the waters rolled back and the slimy riverbed was exposed to the sun. The work began.

Ts'ai Hsing soon realized that he didn't have enough workers or enough money to pay for more. Without more workmen, this precious opportunity would be lost and the beginnings of the bridge would be washed away when the waters returned. Desperate, he called out to Kuan Yin.

A boat appeared downstream, with the White Kuan Yin at the prow, lovely as the sun and the moon. Her presence drew flocks of people from the surrounding country. Her words flowed over them like clear streams or wind in the trees. Every man immediately fell in love with her. Then Kuan Yin said: 'I will marry the man who throws gold or silver in my lap.' Showers of gold and silver descended on her. The boat was soon full to overflowing. But not one coin fell in her lap.

She gave the money to Ts'ai Hsing, who hired five thousand more workers and doubled their wage. The foundations were completed just one hour before the turbulent waters returned.

The stories of Kuan Yin's Miracles and Healings are innumerable and are added to each day. Every shrine is full of votive objects that tell a story about her compassion and her power to break the inexorable chain of suffering. Kuan Yin can change your fate.

In this tradition, fate is not an implacable destiny written in stone. It is a subtle set of potentials, possibilities and boundaries that define a personality. Fate says that you will be born rich or poor, female or male, healthy or weak, but it does not say what you will do with it. You have a basic character represented by certain symbolic animals. Key meetings and events are indicated. All this is the result of karma, past actions and experiences and emotions that can shape future events. However, the chain of karma can be broken or re-shaped at any time. A change of heart or a change of awareness will change your fortune for good or bad. This change of heart is effected by acts of kindness, compassion and insight. It is often brought about by the intervention of the Great Protectors and their transfer of spiritual force and merit.

In one miracle story, a monk saw the signs of death clearly written on the face of a young boy who had come to ask if he should take a long journey to see his parents. The monk advised him to go, thinking that the boy would die happily in his family's arms. But the boy returned and the signs on his face had completely changed. Now they said he would live a long and happy life. What happened?

On his journey, the boy crossed a flooded river and spontaneously saved a group of ants trapped by the waters. For his compassion for the fate of the myriad beings, his own fate was changed.

Another modern story tells of a rich and powerful man who had given up his ideals in the fulfillment of his ambitions. One day, he caused an accident. Two people were killed and he was completely paralyzed, alive yet trapped in an inert body. Acknowledging his foolish and greedy behavior, he called on Kuan Yin, the Compassionate One. She appeared to him, clothed in white light and, like Asklepios in the Greek healing temples, touched his face, neck, arms, hands and chest and then disappeared. He reached out to her in sorrow as she left and suddenly realized he could move!

In another modern story, a young man was climbing in the mountains, his heart troubled and angry at what he felt was a great betrayal. He took a dangerous trail across a cliff face, a narrow ledge with a wire stretched along it at chest level. It began to rain. The rocks grew treacherous. Suddenly the ledge crumbled and he faced a long fall to certain death on the rocks below. He called to Kuan Yin and time stopped as she appeared. A hand firmly took his and put it on the wire. Another hand touched his heart. Weeping in gratitude, he made his way across the cliff, saved from death and lasting bitterness.

Kuan Yin also inspired the well-loved tale of Monkey or The Journey to the West, a famous historical romance written about the journey of the monk Hsuan Tsang (596–664 CE) to India to bring Buddhist scriptures of revelation and liberation back to China.[19] The novel was written by Wu Ch'eng-en in sixteenth century Huai-nan, drawing on an immense background of histories, legends and stage plays.

Monkey is a mix of folk tale, poetry, religion, allegory, history and political satire. The Heavenly Saints are the bureaucrats, for the Chinese people were well aware that the 'Heaven' they heard so much about was the bureaucratic system that ruled them transferred upwards.

The other title of the novel is *The Journey to the West*, for the West in Chinese thought is the source of enlightenment and the location of paradise. Tripitaka, the monk-hero who 'leads' the journey is an Ordinary Person like you or me, blundering his way anxiously through life's difficulties. He is sent by the Goddess to bring back scriptures of Greater Vehicle Buddhism from the Great Thunderbolt Monastery in India, home of the Buddha Tathagata. For in Kuan Yin's words, the Lesser Vehicle scriptures 'cannot carry the souls of the dead', while the Greater Vehicle will carry the dead to heaven, save all those in trouble and deliver all those who trust in it from the comings and goings of birth and re-birth. Buddha entrusted the carrying out of this mission to Kuan Yin, telling her to 'reform any demons you meet and send them to help this poor monk'.

In the beginning, all of Tripitaka's helpers are imprisoned or in exile in the fallen world. Monkey, the main figure and guide, represents the restless intensity of our creative genius that is stabilized and focused by the Goddess. Here is his original boast as he tries to take over the Green Jade Heaven:

Born of sky and earth, fused with immortal magic,
I am an old monkey from the Flower Fruit Mountain.
I ply my trade in the Water Curtain Cave.
I found a friend and master who taught me the Great Secret.
I made myself perfect in the Immortality Arts.
I learned transformations without boundaries.
I got tired of this narrow human life
And decided to live in the Green Jade Heaven.

Why should they always have the same master?
Move over, Heavenly Emperor, king must succeed king.
The strong yields to the stronger.
The real hero, like me! Vies with the greatest powers.

On hearing this, Buddha bursts out laughing. After a contest in which he fails to jump free of the Buddha's world-embracing palm, Monkey is imprisoned in Five Element Mountain to purify himself and await Kuan Yin's monk Tripitaka.

Pigsy or, to use his full name, Pigsy Bristles, is the second companion of the monk Tripitaka. He represents our desires and appetites. A monumental eater, he is a former inhabitant of Heaven who was in command of the Watery Hosts. He was expelled to earth after a scandalous episode with the Moon Goddess and fitted out with a pig body, though he retains his magic powers. Kuan Yin encountered him and converted him, setting him up in the Cloud Ladder Cave to await the coming of the pilgrim Tripitaka.

Sandy, the third companion, is a fierce monster living at the bottom of the River of Flowing Sands, where 'a goose feather will not float and a rush flower sinks straight to the bottom'. This is the world without foundations where nothing has identity or permanence, the world of everyday life. Huge-tusked Sandy eats travelers and fishermen on the river and wears a necklace of nine skulls. He was once a Heavenly Alchemist who broke a precious crystal glass and was exiled to the Flowing Sands. He, too, has been converted and put here by Kuan Yin to respond to the pilgrim's call. The Nine-Skull Necklace, sign of his sins, is arranged into a magic square that ferries the travelers across the treacherous River of Sand.

Kuan Yin gives Tripitaka three headbands that he can use to control his three unruly disciples, particularly Monkey. The journey is not easy. Again and again Monkey's radical interventions are required. Kuan Yin, too, intervenes often to restore order. After many harrowing metaphysical adventures and misadventures, they return with the scriptures and all receive enlightenment, transformed without losing their real nature or fate. For Kuan Yin is the companion on our voyage of life. She works in and through each of our hearts to save us from death and the compulsions of karma.

THE DIVINER'S COMPASS[20]

A very famous passage from the *Tao te ching*, a fifth century BCE classic of philosophical Taoism, states that: The *Tao* (Way) gave birth to the One; the One gave birth to the Two; the Two gave birth to the Three; and the Three gave birth to the Ten Thousand Things. This sequence was as well known and as revered in traditional China as the western God's pronouncement 'Let there be light!' The Way or *tao*, what has been called the 'on-going process of the Real', cannot be captured in words. It spontaneously brings forth the One, the Great Unity of all things. The One, in turn, gives birth to the Two, the Primal Powers of Dark and Light, Yin and Yang, expressed as two kinds of lines. Now there are Three: Unity and the Two Powers constantly transforming themselves into each other. Together they create all the things we see and experience in the world we live in, the All–Under–Heaven.

Diviners tried to find ways to describe the interaction of the Two Powers and the chains of dynamic processes that they create. If they could do that, they would be able to intuit where and how the energy was moving and work with it consciously. They would be moving with the Way, in itself a very great good. Further, anything you want to do stands a much greater chance of success if it is working with these energies rather than against them.

The first step was to collect the properties that define the mysterious Two Powers. Some of these contrasting sets of qualities are described in the table below:

The Two Powers

Yin, the power that constructs, is:	Yang, the power that acts, is:
Water	Fire
Moon	Sun
Lower	Upper
Inside	Outside
Dark	Bright
Moist	Dry
Soft	Hard
Hidden	Clear
Contracts	Expands
Twisting	Straight
Brings to completion	Begins
Responds	Stimulates
Receives	Initiates
Yields	Persists
Is	Does
The shady south bank of a river	The bright northern bank of a river
The shady north slope of a mountain	The bright southern slope of a mountain
Clouds and moving shadows	Sunrise and bright flags

In the *I Ching* or *Classic of Change*, China's greatest system of Wisdom Divination, and in many other works on divination,

philosophy and cosmology, these two primal powers are represented by two kinds of lines:

⸺ ⸺   ⸺⸺

The Lines, too, have names and special qualities associated with
the Two Powers:

- **Opened** *(yin)*: open up,
  bring out, develop,
  germinate things;
  the womb; Small, flexible,
  pliant, tender, supple;
  adapt to things.

- **Whole** *(yang)*: unite, bring
  together, single purpose,
  focused; the phallus;
  Great, firm, strong,
  unyielding, persisting;
  impose on things.

The oldest words for the Two Powers, **Great** and **Small**, also
connected them with attitudes and stances we should take to
respond to the changing flow of time and the demands of the spirit:

- **Small** *(yin)*: little, humble,
  common; adapt to what
  crosses your path; move
  in harmony with change.
  Small People adjust to
  circumstances flexibly
  and survive the vicissitudes
  of life.

- **Great** *(yang)*: big, noble,
  important, focus your will
  and impose your ideas;
  guide or lead your life.
  Great People impose a rule
  on their lives and use
  their power to protect
  others.

For the Two Powers are never still. They are constantly changing
into each other, and their transformations create the world we see
around and within us. They transform themselves in a particular
rhythm that diviners described by doubling these two kinds of lines.

The resulting Four Figures were mapped against a series of other cyclical qualities, beginning with the seasons and the directions. The names and sequence of the Four Figures come from a very old divinatory formula, *Fundamental Success: Advantageous Divination*, which can also be translated as *Spring Growing: Harvesting Trial*.

The Four Figures

—— ——

Spring

Point of origin, fundamental, source, first sign, generating power; rising, rousing; sexual energy, excite, emerge; flowering; birth, children; emerging yang.

————

Growing (summer)

Completing, pervading, successful, maturing; unfolding; vigorous, effective; fruiting; adults, parents, active people; yang in action.

—— ——

Harvesting (autumn)

Advantageous, profitable, gain, nourishing; reaping, gathering; crops; elders, the old ones; emerging yin.

—— ——

Trial (winter)

Testing, ordeal, proof, divination; enfolding; separating, toiling, dissolving; risk and danger; seed, kernel, pearl; the ancestors, the dead; wisdom; yin in action.

Diviners soon integrated another system with the Cycle of the Four Figures, a system called the Five Processes or Elements (*wu hsing*): Wood, Fire, Earth, Metal and Water. These five interact in various ways to *produce* and *control* one another.

The Five Processes

Wood
Organic growth, origins, beginnings, east, spring, dawn; sprouting, pushing through, germinate; green plants, shoots.
Wood *produces* Fire. Fire *controls* Wood.

Fire
Burning, heat, light, flames, burning and consuming; summer, south, noon, scarlet; spreading, glowing.
Fire *produces* Earth. Earth *controls* Fire.

Earth
Soil, ground, ashes; yielding and producing; the pivot of the day and night, yellow; sowing and reaping, crops and harvests.
Earth *produces* Metal. Metal *controls* Earth.

Metal
Crystallizing, concentrating, coagulating; autumn, west, sunset, white and indigo; melting and casting into forms.
Metal *produces* Water. Water *controls* Metal.

Water
Fluids, flowing; rivers, streams, floods; winter, north, midnight, black; leveling, equalizing, dissolving difference and form.
Water *produces* Wood. Wood *controls* Water.

By superimposing one cycle on the other, making Earth the common center for all, the diviners made a new diagram that included directions, seasons, processes and their fundamental divinatory meanings. A new Compass was born.

The Diviner's Compass

1

Spring

East, Sunrise, Wood; emerging yang;
sexual energy, excite, emerge; children.

2

Growing (summer)

South, Noon, Fire, yang in
action; successful, mature;
fruits; adults, parents.

4

Trial (winter)

North, Midnight, Water, yin
in action; testing, ordeal,
proof; seeds; ancestors.

3

Harvesting (autumn)

West, Sunset, Metal, emerging yin;
advantageous, profitable, gain; crops; elders, the Old Ones.

The final element added to this Compass was the Eight Diagrams (*pa gua*) from the *Classic of Change*. These eight three-line figures form another cycle of actions and qualities that describes the nature of the energy creating a given moment of time (*shi*).

The Eight Diagrams

Shake
One whole line beneath two opened lines.
The rousing power of **Thunder** that fertilizes everything in
the early spring. Things emerge from eggs and buds;
people are filled with energy and inspiration.

Ground
One opened line beneath two whole lines.
The gentle power of **Wind** and **Wood** that penetrates
and nourishes things as spring progresses. Things expand
and grow, sending out branches, leaves and roots; people
come together in couples to begin a new generation.

Radiance
One opened line between two whole lines.
The spreading power of **Brightness** and **Fire** that rises in
high summer.
Things mature and bear fruit; people come together in
groups and realize they must help one another.

Field
Three opened lines.
The **Earth** that is mother of all. It nourishes all things
and brings them forth into the world, inspiring people
to undertake difficult tasks together.

Open
One opened line above two whole lines.
The fertile and joyous power of the **Mists**, the Marshes
and the Lakes that emerges as the autumn harvest assures
us of plenty. It stimulates and cheers. People laugh
and talk and barter together.

Force
Three whole lines.
Heaven, father of us all. It is the creative spirit, dynamic and enduring, that brings light and rain, inspiring people to struggle to bring forth new things.

Gorge
One whole line between two opened lines.
The brave and venturesome power of the **Stream,** rushing between the narrow walls of a ravine. It takes us through the ordeal of winter. People toil at heavy labor.

Bound
One whole line above two opened lines.
The steadfast power of the **Mountain** that sets limits and articulates things. People become still and quiet in order to see into the mysteries.

All of these symbols and categories describe the on-going dynamic processes of the world both inside and outside us. They formed the basis of traditional culture, offering an insight into how the world works and how we find a place in it.

In the *Oracle of Kuan Yin*, these basic categories are further keyed and organized around Four Moon Phases: Waxing, Full, Waning and Dark. Each of the Divinatory Poems is connected to one of these phases. This connection lets you feel the kind of energy that is underlying your situation: rising, radiant, contracting or hidden. It lets you see in which direction this energy is flowing: spring to summer, summer to autumn, autumn to winter, winter to spring or, in moon language, waxing to full, full to waning, waning to dark, dark to waxing. You will find one of these Four Moon Phases attached to each of Kuan Yin's *100 Divinatory Poems*:

The Moon Phases

Waxing Moon: Emerging Yang
This is the source of energy and power, the origin of sexual drives.
Use it to unfold your plans. Rouse things, help them emerge and
flower. Free yourself and play.
Season: Spring & the East *Element*: Wood
Symbols: Thunder, Wind & Wood
Life Cycle: birth & childhood

Full Moon: Yang in Action
Everything grows, matures and ripens, vigorous and effective.
Unfold and complete your plans and watch them bear fruit. Care
for the children.
Season: Summer & the South *Element*: Fire
Symbols: Brightness & Warmth
Life Cycle: adults, parents

Waning Moon: Emerging Yin
This is the time to harvest. It will bring insight as well as profit.
Reap and gather your crops. Conserve your energy and nourish the
spirits. Honor the experienced.
Season: Autumn & the West *Element*: Metal
Symbols: Mists & Heaven
Life Cycle: the Elders

Dark Moon: Yin in Action
Put things to the proof, submit to the ordeal, separate wheat from
chaff by divination. This is the time of the seed and the hidden
pearl. Rely on the Ancestors' wisdom.
Season: Winter & the North *Element: Water
Symbols: Stream & Mountain
Life Cycle: ancestors, the Old Ones, the dead

These images reflect the presence of Kuan Yin's shining pearlescent orb, shedding the light of compassion even on the darkest night. They are another of her gifts to help you orient yourself in the moving world and feel the joy in its continual dance of energies and images.

Empowering the Oracle

In his foreword to the *I Ching* or *Classic of Change*, the psychologist C. G. Jung openly consulted the oracle and took its advice quite seriously, much to the horror of his translator Cary Baynes. The reading, in which the *I Ching* gave a very coherent and insightful answer to his question about its progress in the West, was the centerpiece of the introduction. At the end of the piece, Jung remarked:[21]

> Any person of clever and versatile mind can of course turn the whole thing around and show how I have projected my subjective contents into the symbols of the hexagrams. Such a critique, though catastrophic from the standpoint of Western rationality, does no harm to the function of the *I Ching*. On the contrary, the Chinese Sage would smilingly tell me, 'Don't you see how useful the *I Ching* is in making you project your hitherto unrealized thoughts into its abstruse symbolism? You could have written your foreword without ever realizing what an avalanche of misunderstanding might be released by it.'

This quality that Jung calls 'projection' or 'transference' seems to play a key role in the relation between an oracle and an inquirer. Jung defined this projection as the transfer of a subjective process onto an object. This transfer is based on an 'archaic identity' of that subject and object. It can be passive, that is unconscious, and get us into quite a bit of trouble. Or it can be active, a kind of 'feeling-into' that brings you into an intimate relation with the object or 'other'. The object, in this case the oracle, is 'animated' by this transference and connected to your feelings and experience.

We usually 'project' certain parts of our deep unconscious processes, personified parts that Jung calls the archetypal images. In the case of the oracle, this projective bridge seems to be an archetypal process called the Old Wise Person, a form of our deep self. When it is activated, it creates a numinous aura around the answers and sets up a field in which 'synchronous' events occur, events and experiences that link inner and outer worlds.

This archetypal field offers a reasonable analogy to what the Chinese thinkers called the Sage Mind. The emotional field around this archetype is a source of synchronicity. It possesses qualities of a parapsychological nature, relativizes space and time and behaves as though it were not localized in one person.

The projection or field of the Wise Old Person establishes a connection; the immediate charge to the oracle comes from a specific affect or emotion in the inquirer that is experienced as a problem, difficulty or dilemma. According to Jung, such difficulty often occurs because your conscious mind has become too rigid. The unconscious parts that have been excluded or repressed 'constellate' or come together as an image loaded with affect or emotion. As the unconscious image emerges into consciousness, you find yourself in an objective situation that somehow coincides with it. The oracle then helps you search for the *meaning*, the connection between outer situation and inner emotion.

The emotion is focused by the diviner and inquirer and transferred to the oracle through a question. This activates the oracle, which returns the emotion to you as a symbol, a 'counter-transference' that has the ability to change your conscious attitude. It can oppose, modify or re-enforce the desire you articulated in your question, thus giving your unconscious a voice. By doing this, it suggests a whole new balance between conscious and unconscious and points at a new center of personality. This is a *mirroring* transference and counter-transference. It therapeutically mirrors your situation and your identity. This reflects our lifelong human need to be seen, to have our identity validated. It gives the deep self a voice in the events of everyday life.

This mirroring works itself out in the 'matching' (*dang*) that fits the symbol that you received from the oracle to your individual situation. It is an intuitive, not a rational procedure. The way it arranges facts, feelings and images duplicates the way your imagination creates the reality you experience each day of your life.

Beginning the Dialogue

In order to talk with Kuan Yin, you must have a question and a way of generating at random a series of numbers between 1–100. The question should be something that is of personal concern. There are several ways to generate the numbers. This 'chance' method is thought to give the spirits and the voice of the unconscious a chance to pick the symbol that opens communication. The important thing in all these methods is that you do not have conscious control of the choice. Jung called this *synchronicity*, the coincidence of meaning in a certain moment of time.

The **Sticks of Fate** is the traditional way. This method involves a tall narrow cup, often a joint from a large bamboo, filled with a hundred thin bamboo slats. They are red on one end and have a number and a character on the other. You hold and gently shake the cup from side to side until one stick pops out, then look up the number in the *100 Poems*.

If you are not acquainted with the *100 Poems* and wish to try the oracle right now, you can form a question and **Think of a Number** or numbers at random.

You can also make a **Divining Bowl** by using a hundred similar balls, squares or pieces of wood or paper, inscribing them with the numbers 1–100, and picking them out of a bowl at random. A simpler version uses ten counters with the numbers 0–9 inscribed on them. In this case you pick *twice* to reach a number, letting 00 stand for one hundred.

Yet another method is a **Chart**, a large piece of paper with a hundred circles drawn on it, numbered 1–100. Close your eyes and put your finger on the paper, then open your eyes and note the number.

You do not have to limit yourself to one number. Kuan Yin's Oracle is extremely flexible in this regard. You can open a dialogue by asking further questions on the same theme. You can ask for images of various alternatives. You can make a reading for someone distant or a group can ask a question together. You can also make what diviners call 'spreads', setting up a structure of meaning then finding numbers to go in each place. A quite interesting 'spread' consists of one number for the Overall Situation, one number each for Past, Present and Future, and another number as a Summary. Feel free to come up with others.

Overall

Past   **Present**   **Future**

Summary

Some say that you should only use a reading if one number is shaken out of the cup. Others, and I am of this school, believe that the two or three sticks that may jump out at the same time can give a very interesting progression or series of viewpoints. Similarly, if you ask a question using a method other than the Sticks of Fate, don't hesitate to draw several numbers on or around the area you are investigating. Kuan Yin has great patience with this and, as long as you accord her a basic respect and affection, she will seldom refuse to speak with you.

Similarly, though there is no need for an elaborate ritual when using the oracle, there are a few basic procedures that help create a sympathetic imaginative space that indicates you are open and ready to receive communication. In an emergency, Kuan Yin will answer with no preparation at all. However, it is often good to set off a little time and space, calm your speeding mind and, if you care to, visualize yourself entering one of her landscapes: a temple, a mountain ledge or cave, a grotto, a cliff above the black night sea with the pearl of the moon shining on the water. You will easily find your own place in the imagination. Then think of the question you wish to have answered, throw or pick the numbers and open her Book of Fates.

When you turn to Kuan Yin's *100 Poems*, you will find a set of complex symbols with several parts, each of a different style or nature. These symbols really come to life only in a specific context, so here is an example that may suggest how you can read them. A woman was involved, against her will, in a complex struggle for power in the company she worked for. Factions formed. The outcome, still unknown, would have a profound effect on her and a project she was deeply involved with. She asked how to deal with the situation. Here is the symbol Kuan Yin used to answer her:

• 17 TURN A DEAF EAR

> Turn a deaf ear to scandal and gossip.
> When you believe lies and deceptive words,
> it is as if you tried to still your hunger
> by eating the picture of a cake.

> *Waxing Moon: Emerging Yang*
> This is the source of energy and power, the origin of sexual
> drives. Use it to unfold your plans. Rouse things, help them
> emerge and flower. Free yourself and play.
> *Season*: Spring & the East *Element*: Wood
> *Symbols*: Thunder, Wind & Wood
> Life Cycle: birth & childhood

If you can free yourself of illusions, envy and greed, this will be a very
fertile and creative time.

What Can and Cannot Happen

- Your family is very turbulent now, so concentrate on making it better.
- You have a clear field in business. Don't let trivial obstacles bother you. Creative energy is on the rise.
- Your relationship is troubled, but a heart-to-heart talk will clear things up.
- If you are expecting a child, the birth will be uncomplicated.
- If you are caught in legal struggles, don't be unyielding. A friendly reconciliation is better than going to court.
- Don't change your home, even if you feel uncomfortable. You would soon find yourself in a very difficult situation.
- Don't worry about your illness. If you are patient, it will soon be cured.

Advice to the Wayfarer

Once you are caught in the whirlpool of scandal and gossip, you will be dragged deeper and deeper until you forget your own plans. Turn a deaf ear! These stories are deception that breed vanity and emptiness. If you eat that cake, you only swallow hunger. Be realistic about your family, your relationship and your opportunities. Don't be influenced by outside advisors. Don't take risks unless you are convinced that the plan is feasible. **Dharma**: find the center and stay on the way.

The basic image is the four-line **Poem** at the head of the page. You should let the poem resonate through all the parts of your situation without immediately trying to analyze it. The poem gave the inquirer a vivid warning about the futility of identifying with any of the factions involved. It would only feed an insatiable appetite for illusion. The poem is combined with a description of the **Moon Phase**, taken from the Diviner's Compass, that told her that the time was actually full of creative energy, the birth of new beings. She should rouse and stimulate things in her work to new growth. Taken together, these two texts gave her a specific piece of advice. They told her to ignore the factions, illusions that created nothing but negative emotion, and concentrate completely on her own project.

The section titled **What Can and Cannot Happen** is full of specific applications. You choose those that are relevant to your specific question and ignore the rest. She chose:

- You have a clear field in business. Don't let trivial obstacles bother you. Creative energy is on the rise, so get excited.
- If you are caught in legal struggles, don't be unyielding. A friendly reconciliation is better than going to court.
- Don't change your home, even if you feel uncomfortable. You would soon find yourself in a very difficult situation.

All of these spoke directly to her question and her situation. The final section **Advice to the Wayfarer** has the tone of a heart-to-heart talk with someone who knows you and the situation. It warned her against becoming caught in a whirlpool of scandal and gossip and encouraged her to be realistic about her family, relationship and opportunities. This section ends in a suggestion called **Dharma**, a spiritual thought or practice that can help you change your thinking on the problem.

All together, these texts gave the woman involved a clear and inspiring way to handle a difficult situation. They freed her from anxiety and enabled her to navigate the difficult waters without being pulled into the whirlpools of illusion. In the end, she and her project not only emerged unscathed but prospered.

The poems numbered 84, 86, 90, 91 and 100 are deemed Special Fate poems and are indicated by the ⟡ symbol. These poems have no 'What Can and Cannot Happen' section because there is no such information provided in the Chinese original. They would seem to indicate that a special destiny or special moment that cuts through normal circumstances is involved in the question or situation that you brought to the oracle. Thus you can count on the aid of the spirits in all circumstances. They will carry you through.

KEYWORDS AND IDEAS

The following words and the ideas or experiences they represent are often used or implicitly referred to in the *Oracle of Kuan Yin*. Together, they help you understand what Kuan Yin says and how she says it.

Afflictive or negative emotions are addictive mental mechanisms based on the false view that we are only a greedy ego that must defend itself against others. They include ignorance or wrong thinking, greed, hate, envy and self-righteousness. By changing the way we see ourselves and our relation to the world of the spirit, we can be freed from the endless suffering caused by these emotions. The greatest liberator is compassion.

Avalokitesvara: Male form of Kuan Yin described in the Lotus Sutra, much revered in Tibetan Buddhism. The Dalai Lama is considered to be an incarnation of Avalokitesvara.

Bodhisattva, Bodhisattva Vow: People who take the Way of the Bodhisattva make a Vow to achieve enlightenment for the happiness of all sentient beings, refusing to accept liberation until all can be liberated. They realize that this is the only way they can ameliorate human suffering. Over the course of many lives they achieve enlightenment, but remain in the Worlds of Becoming to help struggling humans. Bodhisattvas emanate a great compassion and insight. Many take specific vows. Kuan Yin has vowed to come to the aid of anyone who calls on her with a sincere heart.

Buddha: a perfectly enlightened being, with all necessary knowledge and complete development of universal compassion. She or he can manifest in any form or at any time to help other beings free themselves from suffering. Buddhists feel that Buddhahood is the goal of evolution and is attainable by every human being.

Change, *Classic of Change (I Ching)*: Change (*i* or *yi*) describes the constant movement and transformation of all things. The *Classic of Change (I Ching)*, the world's oldest and most profound system of wisdom divination, organizes the images of this way of transformation so that we can read and participate in it.

Detach/dis-identify: the ability, often cultivated through spiritual practices and insights, to separate yourself from the compulsive action of both negative emotions and conventional ideas of reality. This can make the mind much more flexible and life much more enjoyable for you and those around you. These practices are central to Taoist and Buddhist Paths.

Dharma: Teaching, Doctrine or Law. The Dharma is a set of practices and ideas that compose a path that can lead to enlightenment. They evolve in a series of 'turnings' (turning the Wheel of Dharma) that reveal different facets of the Way. The basis of the Dharma is the **Four Noble Truths**: the truth of suffering, the truth of the origin of suffering, the truth of the cessation of suffering and the truth of the path.

Divination/oracle: the art of revealing what is hidden, the sources, powers, motivations and processes that shape what we experience. The symbols of a divination system seek to open a dialogue with these powers, allowing the spirits to reshape the way we are thinking. An oracle is a person or process that gives the spirits a voice.

Dragon: embodiment of spirit energy, at once creative and destructive. The Dragon holds up the dwellings of the gods, brings the fertilizing rain, conceals and confers the pearl of knowledge, the treasure hard to obtain.

Family: in Kuan Yin's Oracle, family refers to those immediately related to you by blood, ties of affection or binding ceremonies.

Fate/destiny: a subtle set of potentials, possibilities and boundaries that define a personality. Fate says that you will be born rich or poor, female or male, healthy or weak, indicates key events and meetings but does not say what you will do with these things. It is the result of karma, past actions, experiences and emotions that have the power to shape future events. The chain of karma or fate can be broken. A change of heart or a change of awareness can change your fortune for good or ill. This change of heart is effected by acts of kindness, compassion and insight or the reverse. It is also brought about by the intervention of the Great Protectors and their transfer of spiritual merit.

Heaven-and-Earth, All-Under-Heaven: in Chinese thought, Heaven-and-Earth (*T'ien-Ti*) mark the bounds of the world, encompassing everything. The All-under-Heaven (*T'ien hsia*) is the world we live in, the world of the Myriad Beings or Ten Thousand Things. One image for Heaven-and-Earth was a Great Turtle swimming through the fertile seas of chaos. The upper shell is Heaven, the lower is Earth and we are the soft flesh in between.

Household: in Kuan Yin's Oracle, household indicates the extended family, including dependants, relations, animals and key friends, while the family is the core, related by blood, deep affection or binding ceremonies.

Kairos: Greek word for a hole in the fabric of time, a critical moment when we can move between worlds or make significant changes. Divinatory symbols (*hsiang*) can create such a kairos. Chinese diviners call them Dragon Holes or 'Moments' in Time (*shi*).

Kannon/Kwannon: Kuan Yin's name in Japan, where in particular she developed the art of dream incubation.

Karma: Karma means 'action', actions that in turn become motivations. That a flower is a flower and I am a human is not karma, but natural law. When the existence of these things causes experiences of happiness or pain, karma is involved. Karma is the imprint of previous emotional experience that conditions and shapes how we currently experience things.

Moment: see Kairos.

Om Mane Padme Hum: called the Jewel in the Lotus, this is the basic mantra of Kuan Yin and Avalokitesvara. **Om** invokes the universal divine; **Mani** is the jewel of great compassion; **Padme** is the lotus of the wisdom of selflessness; **Hum** is the integration of all in the individual mind.

Samsara is the Tomb World or World of Illusions, the unenlightened life of humans and other beings. It implies an endless round of suffering caused by living in the impossible situation of feeling yourself a separate individual up against an infinite and hostile universe.

Significant Relationship: in Kuan Yin's Oracle, a mutual bonding of two people based on affection, referred to as marriage in traditional cultures. It indicates the primary emotional relationship in your life, one that endures through time and change. You must commit yourself to such a relationship.

Skillful means: literally: expedient, stratagem, device, craft, art, language. Skillful means (*upaya*) is synonymous with love (*karuna*). It is the 'father' of the Bodhisattva Way, the means through which enlightenment is unfolded to the Myriad Beings in order to relieve the sufferings of attachment. There is one truth, but many ways or skillful means. One of the greatest of these skillful means is divination.

Sticks of Fate: the Sticks of Fate (*chien tung*) are the traditional method of consulting the Oracle of Kuan Yin. They consist of a narrow cup made from the joint of a bamboo and a hundred thin slats, red on one end and numbered on the other. You shake the cup until one of the slats jumps out. The number on the bottom indicates a text in Kuan Yin's Book of Oracles.

Symbolizing: a symbol (*hsiang*) is an image that has the power to connect things. In divination, it connects the visible world of your problem to the invisible world of the spirit. We use divination to *hsiang* things, to turn them into symbols and symbolic awareness. A *hsiang* can be a magic spell, a likeness, a pattern or model. You can *hsiang* or enter the symbolic process by imagining, creating images, imitating, acting, playing or writing. We make the connection between the invisible world of the spirit and the visible world of our lives by playing with symbols, by imitating them and acting them out.

Tara: Tibetan form of Kuan Yin. Tara is the Great Goddess as protector and redeemer who proclaims: 'I take my worshipers across the ocean of dangers!' She 'happily leads us out' (*Tarati iti Tara*) of dangerous defiles and menacing terrors. She is 'mistress of boats', served by a flock of women who rescue the shipwrecked. Like Kuan Yin, she is the *shakti* or power of Avalokitesvara and is worshiped as *Prajna Paramita*, mother of all Buddhas and spiritual perfections.

Tao means 'way' or 'path.' In its oldest uses it denotes either a literal road or the life and behavior of a particular kind of person: a carpenter's *tao*, a wife's *tao*, a warrior's *tao*. It developed into the most fundamental, mysterious and attractive term in Eastern thought. As the 'on-going process of the real', it traces a path for the entire universe and, at the same time, for each individual being in it. To be 'in' *tao* is to be connected to the source of meaning and value. It is a religious experience of a high order. It brings joy, connection, spontaneity, creativity and compassion.

Te can be translated as power and virtue or potency. Closely associated with *tao*, it is the power or virtue that allows something to fully exist, a realizing power that people can accumulate and nurture. Powerful *te* makes a powerful person. Exalted *te* makes a wise person or sage. Someone full of *te* is numinous because they have the power to realize *tao* in their person. By accumulating and refining *te*, you become 'great', that is, able to lead your own life.

Three Refuges or **Three Jewels** are the Buddha, the Dharma and the Sangha. People take refuge in the Three Jewels 'until enlightenment comes' because they fear to be reborn again and again in the states of woe. The Buddha found the way to freedom, taught the Dharma that way and founded the Sangha or community of seekers.

Transformation (*hua*) is a radical change of form. It marks a quantum change of energy, the move from one state of being to another. It is often coupled with another term meaning gradual change to produce the phrase *p'ien hua*, change and transformation. Transformation is of great interest to diviners, for the behavior of things in transitional states is exactly what they want to understand. If you locate a transformation, you know precisely where and how change is taking place.

Transfer of Merit: in Kuan Yin's Oracle, care and concern are described in terms of the Bodhisattva Vow, the vow to postpone liberation and remain in the world 'for the happiness of all sentient beings'. The Bodhisattvas accumulate vast funds of spiritual merit that they can freely transfer to others (*parinamana*) to aid in their salvation. Because Kuan Yin, who sponsors the oracle, is a Bodhisattva with unlimited Spiritual Merit, she can transfer or 'download' spiritual merit to you through the gate of the symbols. In turn, she will take on or 'upload' your entanglements, releasing you from these knots through her enlightened awareness. This 'reality therapy' breaks the karmic chain of cause and effect and frees you from the compulsion that got you into your tangle in the first place. You 'see through' what is going on and acquire the power to navigate it. This opens the gate to the Pure Land or Western Paradise.

Trishna: Soul does not 'enter' new bodies, but creates forms suitable to its 'thirst' (*trishna*). This thirst is the root of reincarnation and the workings of karma. Trishna brings things into existence. It works wrongly only when it relies on the greedy ego and its ambitions as the principle of life. When freed from these narrow attachments, it becomes aware of the all-knowing and all-loving Compassionate One. This sets up a 'frame of faith' that turns you toward the Pure Land and its Goddess and turns her toward you. Then trishna will work its own way. It becomes *mahakaruna*, the Great Compassion of the Bodhisattva.

Wu-wei (not-acting) or **wu-nien** (not-thinking) is the fundamental tool for coming into contact with the way or *tao*. It relies on the ability to dis-identify with compulsive passions, collective ideas and egotistic ambitions. You create an empty space within and, if you keep it empty, the *tao* will appear in the fertile void. You move only when an impulse to act comes from this empty center. In this way you can act in harmony with the *tao* and can spread peace rather than the conflict of battling egos. Without this capacity, what you do will come to nothing, because you will only act out of your ego and its greedy hunger. The end result of your actions will inevitably be the opposite of what you want.

Yin and yang are the Two Powers that generate the world. They are usually described in terms of contrasting qualities such as dark and light, in and out, water and fire, soft and hard, female and male, yield and persist. 'One light, one dark, is tao' is a famous statement about these powers. In the *Classic of Change*, they are represented by two kinds of lines, **opened** and **whole**, and connect with two attitudes or stances, the **Small** and the **Great**. The Two Powers are constantly changing into each other. Their transformations create the world we see around and within us.

ENDNOTES

Unless otherwise indicated, all translations are my own. I use the old Wade-Giles system of transliteration of Chinese characters to accord with many of my scholarly sources.

[1] The classic description of the Bodhisattva's Way is Shantideva (trans. Batchelor), *Guide to the Bodhisattva's Way of Life*, Dharamsala: LTWA, 1979. A deeply moving explication of this Way is Tensin Gyatso, The Fourteenth Dalai Lama, *A Flash of Lightning in the Dark of Night*, Boston and London: Shambala, 1994. The description of the stages comes from the *Dasabhumika Sutra*. See Har Dayal, *The Bodhisattva Doctrine in Buddhist Sanskrit Literature*, (1932, reprint Delhi, 1970) and Kajiyama Yuichi, 'On the Meaning of the Words Bodhisattva and Mahasattva', in *Indological and Buddhist Studies: Articles in Honor of Professor J. W. de Jong*, ed. L. A. Herman et al., pp. 253-270, Canberra, 1982.

[2] See C. N. Tay, 'Kuan Yin: Cult of Half Asia', *History of Religions* 16, November 1976, pp. 147-177; Alexander Coburn Soper, *Literary Evidence for Early Buddhist Art*, (Ascona, 1959); *Scripture of the Lotus Blossom of the Fine Dharma*, trans. Louis Hurvitz, (New York, 1976); and Henri Maspero, *Taoism and Chinese Religion*, trans. Frank Kierman Jr., (Amherst, 1981), particularly 'The Mythology of Modern China', pps. 166-171.

[3] There are many sources on the Gnostic vision, but I particularly recommend Henri-Charles Puech 'The Concept of Redemption in

Manichaeism', trans. Ralph Mannheim, in *Papers from the Eranos Yearbooks 6*, Princeton: Princeton University Press, Bollingen Series XXX 6, 1968, pp. 247-314; Bentley Layton (trans.), *The Gnostic Scriptures*, London: SCM Press, 1987; and Henri Corbin, *Avicenna and the Visionary Recital*, Dallas: Spring, 1968.

[4] Basic texts on Pure Land are in *Sacred Books of the East*, v.49, 1894, rpt. NY: 1965. See also Henri de Lubac, *Aspects de bouddhisme*, Paris, 1955; Marie-Thérèse de Mallman, *Introduction à l'étude d'Avalokiteçvara*, Paris, 1948; Kenneth Chen, *Buddhism in China*, Princeton: Princeton University Press, 1972 (rpt.); and entries 'Amitaba' and 'Ching'tu' in *Encyclopedia of Religion*, ed. Mircea Eliade, University of Chicago Press.

[5] Translations, commentary and background in Stephen Karcher, *Ta chuan: the Great Treatise*, NY: St Martin's Press, 2000. *Ta chuan* began about 400 BCE as a set of Taoist oral teachings on the use of *Change*. Written down about 175 BCE, it became the central part of the *Ten Wings*, commentary that was added to *Change* in the Han Dynasty. *Ta chuan* was the most important cosmological and spiritual document in post-Han China. Through its re-imagining of the ancient practices of the *wu* or mediums, it turned *Change* into a way of spiritual transformation.

[6] See Stephen Karcher, *The Illustrated Encyclopedia of Divination*, NY: HarperCollins, 2001; 'Oracle's Contexts: Gods, Dreams, Shadow, Language', in *Spring* 53/1992 and 'Which Way I Fly is Hell: Divination in the Shadow of the West', *Spring* 55/1994; Michael Loewe and Carmen Blacker, *Divination and Oracles*, Boulder CO: Shambala, 1981; Philip Peek, ed., *African Divination Systems: Ways of Knowing*, Bloomington IND: Indiana University Press, 1991; Marie-Louise von Franz, *Divination and Synchronicity: The Psychology of Meaningful Chance*, Toronto: Inner City, 1980; Jean-Paul Vernant ed., *Divination et rationalité*, Paris: Editions du Seuil, 1974; and the entry 'Divination' in the *Encyclopedia of Religion*, ed. Mircea Eliade, Chicago: University of Chicago Press.

[7] The *I Ching* is now available in many translations. Unfortunately, many are simply rehashings of old material made without recourse to the Chinese texts. Richard Wilhelm and Cary F. Baynes, *The I Ching or Book of Changes*, (Princeton: Princeton University Press, 1967) is the 'classic' English translation, now badly outdated. Richard John Lynn, *The Classic of Change: The I Ching as interpreted by Wang Bi* (New York: Columbia University Press, 1994) is a translation of the first full Confucian revision of *Change*. For those who can read between the lines it is quite frightening. Wu Jing-Nuan, *Yijing*, (Washington, D.C.: Taoist Study Series, 1991) is an

interesting and usable Taoist version of the oldest parts of the text. Edward Shaugnessy, *I Ching: the Classic of Changes* (The First English Translation of the Newly Discovered Second-Century B. C. *Mawangdui* Texts), New York: Ballantine, 1996 is a scholarly but unusable classic of 'ruthless literal-mindedness'. Cyrille J.-D. Javery, *Le Yi King mot à mot*, Paris: Albin Michel, Series 'Question de' no 98 bis, is another interesting and usable version of the oldest parts of the text. I use Stephen Karcher, *How to Use the I Ching*, NY: HarperCollins, 2001 and *The Classic Chinese Oracle of Change* (with Rudolf Ritsema), NY: HarperCollins, 2001, for both text and background.

[8] Gerard Adler, 'Aspects of Jung's Personality and Work', *Harvest* 21/1975, p.7.

[9] See D. T. Suzuki, *Mysticism: Christian and Buddhist*, London: George Allen & Unwin, 1957, pp. 122-128. The poem from Saichi is cited on page 162.

[10] See Erwin Rouselle, 'Dragon and Mare in Chinese Mythology' (trans. Ralph Mannheim), in *The Mystic Vision: Papers from the Eranos Yearbooks 6*, Princeton: Princeton University Press, 1968; and Marcel Granet, *Danses et légendes de la Chine ancienne*, Paris, 1926, II, pp. 501ff, section *K'ouei*. *Lao t'zu* translations are my own; citation from *Chuang tz'u* is my translation, modified from Rouselle/Mannheim, p. 107.

[11] See *The Classic Chinese Oracle of Change*, pp. 66-67.

[12] *A Flash of Lightning in the Dark Night*, pp. 32-34.

[13] Good translations of basic Taoist texts are: Arthur Waley, *The Way and its Power: A Study of the Tao Te Ching and its Place in Chinese Thought*, London: Unwin 1934, rpt. 1977; Burton Watson, *Complete Works of Chuang Tzu*, New York: Columbia University Press, 1968; and A. C. Graham, *The Book of Lieh t'zu*, London: John Murray, 1960.

[14] Commentary on Taoism includes: John Blofield, *Taoism: The Road to Immortality*, Boston: Shambala, 1985; K. Dean, *Taoist Ritual and Popular Cults of Southeast Asia*, Princeton: Princeton University Press, 1993; Chad Hanson, *A Daoist Theory of Chinese Thought*, New York: Oxford University Press, 1992; L. Kohn, *Early Chinese Mysticism: Philosophy and Soteriology in the Taoist Tradition*, Princeton: Princeton University Press, 1992; Henri Maspero, *Taoism and Chinese Religion*, Amherst: University of Massachusetts Press, 1950/ trans. 1981; Joseph Needham and Wang Ling, 'The *Tao Chia* and Taoism,' in *Science and Civilization in China*, v.2, chap. 1, Cambridge: Cambridge University Press, 1956; Michael Saso, *Taoism and the Rite of Cosmic Renewal*, Pullman WA: Washington State University Press, 1990; and

Holmes Welch and Anna Seidel eds, *Facets of Taoism: Essays in Chinese Religion*, New Haven: Yale University Press, 1979.

[15] Whalen Lai, 'The Interiorization of the Gods', *Taoist Resources*, vol. 1, no. 1, Spring 1985

[16] On Chinese spirit-mediums or *wu*, see J. Paper, *The Spirits are Drunk*: Comparative Approaches to Chinese Religion, Albany: State University of New York, 1995. On contemporary mediums and possession cults see: Roger Bastide, *The African Religions of Brazil*, Baltimore, 1978; J. A. Elliot, *Chinese Spirit-Medium Cults in Singapore*, London, 1955; Jane Belo, *Trance in Bali*, New York, 1960; Erica Bourguignon ed., *Religion, Altered States of Consciousness and Social Change*, Columbus OH: University of Ohio Press, 1973; *Possession*, San Francisco, 1976; and *Trance Dance*, New York, 1968; M. Lewis, *Ecstatic Religion: An Anthropological Study of Spirit Possession and Shamanism*, Harmondsworth: Penguin, 1971; Sheila Walker, *Ceremonial Spirit Possession in Africa and Afro-America*, Leiden: Brill, 1972.

[17] The *Kuan-tz'u* is discussed in A.C. Graham, *Disputers of the Tao: Philosophical Argument in Ancient China*, La Salle IL: Open Court, 1989. See also Whalen Lai, 'The Interiorization of the Gods'. A full translation of the text is now available: Harold D. Roth, *Original Tao: Inward Training and the Foundations of Taoist Mysticism*, NY: Columbia University Press, 1999.

[18] See Lilla Russell-Smith, 'Thousand Buddha Temples of Dunhuang'. (4 parts), *Middle Way*, vol. 70, no.1-4 (May–November, 1995, February 1996) and vol. 71, no. 1 (May 1996); Arthur Waley, 'Avalokitesvara and the Legend of Miao Shan', in *Artibus Asiae* II, Dresden, 1925; Glen Dudbridge, *The Legend of Miao Shan*, Oxford, 1978; M. Palmer, J. Ramsey, M-H. Kwok, *Kuan Yin*, London & San Francisco: Harper Thorsons, 1995.

[19] Arthur Waley (trans.), *Monkey*, Harmondsworth: Penguin, 1961 (excerpts); and A.C. Yu (trans.), *Journey to the West* 4 vol., Chicago: University of Chicago Press, 1977 (complete). The citation is modified from Waley, p. 83.

[20] See *The Classic Chinese Oracle of Change*, pp. 65–86 and bibliography. On thought and culture in traditional China, see Marcel Granet, *La pensée chinoise*, Paris: Albin Michel, 1934; J. M. M. de Groot, *The Religious System of China*, 6 volumes, 1892–1910, rpt. Taipei, 1967; Henri Maspero, *China in Antiquity*, trans. Frank A. Kierman, University of Massachusetts Press, 1978; J. Paper, *The Spirits are Drunk: Comparative Approaches to Chinese Religion*, Albany: State University of New York, 1995; and Benjamin Schwartz, *The World of Thought in Ancient China*, Cambridge MA: Harvard University Press, 1985.

²¹ *I Ching or Book of Changes, The Richard Wilhelm Translation rendered into English by Cary F. Baynes*, Foreword by C.G. Jung, Princeton: Princeton University Press, Bollingen Series xix, 1967, pp. xxxviii–xxxix. Jung's thoughts on projection are from the *Collected Works*, trans. R.F.C. Hull, London: Routledge and Kegan Paul, 1960: CW6, §742-3; CW8, §394, 841, 912; CW10, §849-50; CW11, §1016.

The 100 Poems
of the Goddess

• 1 A LUCKY FATE

Though you have been given a lucky fate,
The time is not yet ripe for you.
Kuan Yin wants to say:
if you are loyal and true, this fate will soon be yours.

(*Waxing Moon: Emerging Yang*

This is the source of energy and power, the origin of sexual drives.
Use it to unfold your plans. Rouse things, help them emerge and
flower. Free yourself and play.
Season: Spring & the East *Element*: Wood
Symbols: Thunder, Wind & Wood
Life Cycle: birth & childhood

---

*The time is not ripe, but energy is rising. You will soon emerge from
the cocoon.*

What Can and Cannot Happen

- Your family and household are in crisis. Get to work and find a solution.
- You can't complain about your business. Next fall and winter you will enjoy an extraordinary success. Creative energy is rising.
- If you want begin a significant relationship, this is the right time.
- If you are expecting a child, it will be a son.
- If you must go to court, have no fear. The judgement will be in your favor.
- If you are sick, don't worry. You will soon be well again.

Advice to the Wayfarer

All the signs are good. Don't let anything get in the way of going through with your plans. You can only win. Be consistent, loyal and true to the Goddess. Think about her qualities constantly! **Dharma**: compassion and insight can change the world you live in.

• 2 YOUNG WHALES

Young whales lie still in the water.
One day when they are grown,
they will leap through the Dragon Door
full of hope.

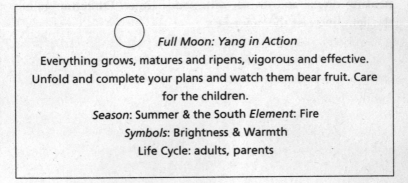

Full Moon: Yang in Action
Everything grows, matures and ripens, vigorous and effective.
Unfold and complete your plans and watch them bear fruit. Care
for the children.
Season: Summer & the South *Element*: Fire
Symbols: Brightness & Warmth
Life Cycle: adults, parents

Lie still, ripen and grow. The leap into life awaits you.

What Can and Cannot Happen

- Your household is shaky now, but things will soon return to peaceful ways.
- Your income will not change, so don't undertake anything to improve it. Don't worry. Creative energy is at your service.
- This is not a good time to begin a significant relationship.
- Conflicts are best settled peacefully now, without recourse to the law.
- Don't worry about your health. There are no problems in store for you.
- If you want to change your home, try the southwest.

Advice to the Wayfarer

Don't be impatient. Don't hurry. Stay still as a young whale as your powers develop. Let everything pass by until your time comes. You have what you need until it is time to emerge. You feel insecure only because the speed of your development doesn't go along with your wishful thinking. Your time will come! Be particularly careful and loving with your partner. **Dharma**: gather the light, increase the inner heat.

• 3 THE TIRELESS SWALLOW

Braving the storm, the traveler finds his way home,
like a tireless swallow that returns to her nest.
But her shelter has crumbled and her work is in vain.
You must begin again.

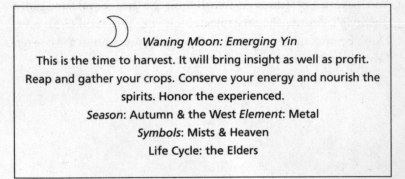

Waning Moon: Emerging Yin
This is the time to harvest. It will bring insight as well as profit.
Reap and gather your crops. Conserve your energy and nourish the
spirits. Honor the experienced.
Season: Autumn & the West *Element*: Metal
Symbols: Mists & Heaven
Life Cycle: the Elders

*Begin again, putting together the fruits of your many experiences. This
will bring you what you need.*

What Can and Cannot Happen

- Things are not going well in your household at the moment, but the signs are good that you can soon restore happiness and harmony.
- Be careful and circumspect in business dealings. Pursue your own professional goals. Don't lose courage. You have more than enough creative energy and ability to conquer this adversity. Gather and concentrate creative energy.
- You must forget your current plans for a significant relationship. Don't be sad, another opportunity will soon arise.
- If you are expecting a child, it will be a son.
- Court and legal proceedings will turn out well.
- A change of home or homeland could be definitely to your

advantage. If you have lost something, don't worry. It will soon be found.

- If you feel under the weather, you will soon have your energy back.

Advice to the Wayfarer

You have fought through many obstacles and stood up against them well. Above all, carry through on your goals and ideals now. Don't be discouraged, for success is waiting just around the corner.
Dharma: resolution, patience and joyous giving.

• 4 THE BROKEN MIRROR

> An old broken mirror, a broken relation,
> can come together again. Reconcile them.
> The pair will live a happy life and found a new home.
> Their happiness will pass onto the children.

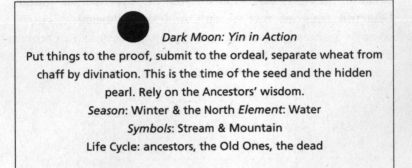

Dark Moon: Yin in Action
Put things to the proof, submit to the ordeal, separate wheat from chaff by divination. This is the time of the seed and the hidden pearl. Rely on the Ancestors' wisdom.
Season: Winter & the North *Element*: Water
Symbols: Stream & Mountain
Life Cycle: ancestors, the Old Ones, the dead

Bring shattered things together again and find the hidden treasure of happiness.

What Can and Cannot Happen

- You have the opportunity to put a precarious relationship on a solid footing through courage and endurance.
- Your business transactions will be successful. You will have a chance to better your finances this fall and winter. Spare no pains. Find the hidden creative energy.
- If you want to begin a significant relationship, you stand under a lucky star.
- Children will come, but after a delay.
- Don't change your home, for your luck lies where you are now. If you have lost something, don't worry. You will find it again.
- Take care of your health, for a lingering illness could develop.

Advice to the Wayfarer

Perseverance and courage will take you to the goal. You have the chance to put your life on a stable basis with a secure future. Be circumspect in all that you do! The effort you spend will be praised in the end, for hard work brings its reward! To find gold you must painstakingly sieve the sand. Be brave. Ride the dragon. Tread on the tiger's tail. Suddenly your great reward will appear. **Dharma**: compassionate strength needs skillful means.

• 5 FINDING THE SPRING

To find a spring, dig deep beneath the grassy surface.
Without effort, you will not win the prize.
A protector will guide you to the blue heavens.
Everything will be easy once these obstacles are conquered.

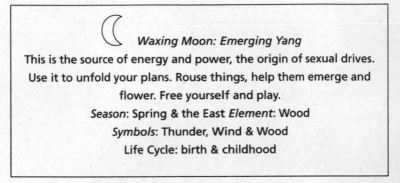

Waxing Moon: Emerging Yang
This is the source of energy and power, the origin of sexual drives.
Use it to unfold your plans. Rouse things, help them emerge and
flower. Free yourself and play.
Season: Spring & the East *Element*: Wood
Symbols: Thunder, Wind & Wood
Life Cycle: birth & childhood

*The source lies beneath the surface. Find it. It is ready to make your life
burst into bloom.*

What Can and Cannot Happen

- Though your household is tense and uncomfortable, if you are careful all will return to peace and satisfaction.
- You temporarily confront many business obstacles. Don't worry. Creative energy is rising.
- Difficulties in your significant relationship will soon vanish of their own accord.
- Expect a child soon!
- The guests you are expecting will be late.
- Don't go to court. Try to settle conflicts in a friendly manner.
- In these circumstances, you should think about changing your home.
- Your illness will last a long time if you don't see a doctor.

Advice to the Wayfarer
A long treasured friendship is bearing fruit now. Someone means
to do well by you and you should take the help that is offered.
Your other difficulties will then be cleared up. Hold back a bit and
people will come to you. **Dharma**: invoke the Great Protectors.

• 6 LIVING WITH THE ANIMALS

Settle down in a hole in the ground and live with the animals.
Be satisfied with what you have and envy no one.
Everyone can stand on their own two feet and make a living,
even if they don't own Heaven and Earth.

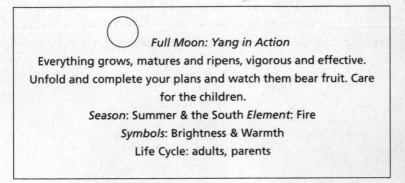

Full Moon: Yang in Action
Everything grows, matures and ripens, vigorous and effective.
Unfold and complete your plans and watch them bear fruit. Care
for the children.
Season: Summer & the South *Element*: Fire
Symbols: Brightness & Warmth
Life Cycle: adults, parents

*All around you the events of your life bear fruit. Enjoy and care for
what you have!*

What Can and Cannot Happen

- Your household is disordered because people have said and done things they don't really mean.
- Though business is disappointing now, success will come in the end. Creative energy is at your service.
- If you want a significant relationship, think carefully while choosing a partner.
- Children will come without complications.
- If you want to change your home, go ahead. It will work to your advantage. You will soon find something that you lost.
- If you don't feel well, go to a doctor just in case.

Advice to the Wayfarer

You are of two minds at the moment, sometimes defensive, sometimes aggressive. Find the balance between the opposites and you will find the strength to get out of your unsatisfactory situation. Don't worry. You can do it when you regain your inner balance. No one will offer you abundance, so you must live simply. Don't lose your joy in life. This situation isn't tragic. Be patient and wait. Let the others fight for riches and power. **Dharma**: distance yourself from the desire for gain. What a blessing it is to be poor!

• 7 THE TURBULENT RIVER

> The river is turgid and clouded.
> If you venture beyond the Great Wall, you will feel uprooted.
> Hold back even when you are ordered to act.
> Don't try to rise and you won't meet misfortune.

)) *Waning Moon: Emerging Yin*

This is the time to harvest. It will bring insight as well as profit.
Reap and gather your crops. Conserve your energy and nourish the
spirits. Honor the experienced.

Season: Autumn & the West *Element*: Metal

Symbols: Mists & Heaven

Life Cycle: the Elders

---

*Caught in a cloudy river of feeling, you must gather and concentrate
your insight.*

What Can and Cannot Happen

- Your household is problematic at present, but the disturbance will soon pass.
- Pursue your goals stubbornly and your business will prosper. This fall and winter, plan to expand your enterprise. Gather and concentrate creative energy.
- Conception and pregnancy now could be complicated and take a long time.
- Plan your trip carefully so you won't be trapped by unforeseen difficulties.
- If you go to court, the judgement will go against you.
- Be careful of your health! Illness could be serious now.

Advice to the Wayfarer

Your situation is unclear and you should plan very carefully. Don't let yourself be influenced by others. You have chosen to do something, so keep to it. When you run into resistance, be flexible. Give way when necessary. Don't be afraid of taking a journey. Find a new place when your ideas are clear. It will bring you to your goal. **Dharma**: the inner journey leads to outer success.

• 8 PINE AND CYPRESS

> Pine and cypress grow and flourish,
> Rain, snow and frost cannot harm them.
> One day, people will use their wood.
> They are the beams and pillars of our world.

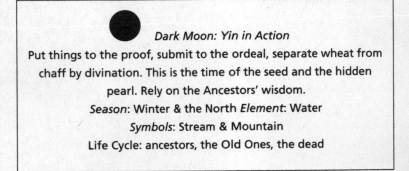

Dark Moon: Yin in Action

Put things to the proof, submit to the ordeal, separate wheat from chaff by divination. This is the time of the seed and the hidden pearl. Rely on the Ancestors' wisdom.

Season: Winter & the North *Element*: Water

Symbols: Stream & Mountain

Life Cycle: ancestors, the Old Ones, the dead

What you are doing now will be the seed of a new life for many. Find the hidden treasure.

What Can and Cannot Happen

- Your household is peaceful and happy. Don't do anything to disturb it.
- You can hope for great career success. Pursue your goals with diplomacy and care. A quick rise in station is certain. Find the hidden creative energy.
- If you are expecting a child, it will be a son.
- If you must go to court, the judgement will be in your favor.
- You will soon have a guest who brings interesting news.
- If you want to change your home, do so. It will bring you a better life.
- If you are sick, don't worry. It won't last long.

Advice to the Wayfarer

People respect and treasure you, so put this to use to further your career. The time has come to talk over the future with your chief. You will soon find an opportune time. Your entire trip will go without problems and you will return to your home full of beautiful memories. **Dharma**: the only true goal is the happiness of all sentient beings.

• 9 THE DARK AND THE LIGHT

Don't let egotism and criticism rule your feelings.
Let your conscience guide you.
Be openhearted, high-minded and exemplary,
as clear as a transparent moon in the heavens of night.

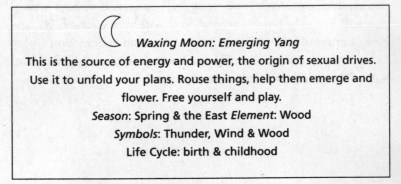

Waxing Moon: Emerging Yang
This is the source of energy and power, the origin of sexual drives.
Use it to unfold your plans. Rouse things, help them emerge and
flower. Free yourself and play.
Season: Spring & the East *Element*: Wood
Symbols: Thunder, Wind & Wood
Life Cycle: birth & childhood

*If you can stay in the middle and keep an open heart, this will be a very
flourishing time.*

What Can and Cannot Happen

- Your household is in order, so treasure it. It will bring you peace and joy.
- Business is only moderately successful, but conditions are ripe for development. Use every chance that is offered. Creative energy is on the rise.
- Plans for a significant relationship will be successful. Everything depends on establishing this on a solid footing.
- If you are expecting a child, it will be a son.
- If you must, go to court with no cares. The judgement will be in your favor.
- A change of home will work greatly to your advantage. If you have lost something, have patience. It will soon be found.

- Take care of your health. Recovery from an illness will be hindered if you don't take enough care.

Advice to the Wayfarer

The time for action has come. Be diplomatic. Weigh each step. Be sure before you make a move. Act out of reflection and thought, not impulse, but don't leave your feelings out. If you go wrong you will not only miss your goal, you will hurt yourself. Be sincere, unprejudiced and impartial. Saints and sages don't play favorites or join factions. This is how we distinguish dark and light. **Dharma**: destroy the greedy ego!

• 10 JADE AND PRECIOUS JEWELS

> What are you doing, seeking riches in foreign lands?
> A treasure of jade and precious jewels lies at your feet.
> It is as if you held a burning lantern
> and went looking for a fire.

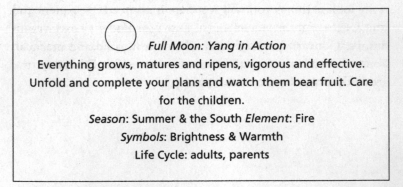

Full Moon: Yang in Action
Everything grows, matures and ripens, vigorous and effective.
Unfold and complete your plans and watch them bear fruit. Care
for the children.
Season: Summer & the South *Element*: Fire
Symbols: Brightness & Warmth
Life Cycle: adults, parents

Why wander? The crop is rich and will soon be ready right here at home.

What Can and Cannot Happen

- Your family is disturbed. Restore the balance as soon as you can.
- Concentrate on your business. You must work very hard to be successful. Creative energy is at your service.
- If you want a significant relationship, don't delay. Waiting is a mistake.
- If you are expecting a child, it will be a daughter.
- The guests you are expecting will soon arrive. They are already on their way.
- Don't go to court. The chances are against you.
- Don't change your home. You have a solid base now. You would only have to rebuild it if you moved.

- If you are sick, be very careful. The illness could last a long time.

Advice to the Wayfarer

You don't really understand your situation. Think it over carefully before you go any further. Though you feel very insecure, if you really look at things you will see there is no need. Be patient and wait for the right moment to act. Don't surrender to extravagant dreams. Concern yourself with what is real, solid and practical. You will suddenly find that you are successful. **Dharma**: the greatest journey begins with one step.

• 11 GOOD LUCK FROM BAD

It is strange to achieve something in the middle of a battle.
As if by magic, an arrow hits a running deer
and what seemed bad luck turns to good.
Whatever you plan will be successful.

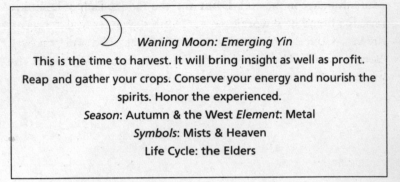

Waning Moon: Emerging Yin

This is the time to harvest. It will bring insight as well as profit.
Reap and gather your crops. Conserve your energy and nourish the
spirits. Honor the experienced.

Season: Autumn & the West *Element*: Metal

Symbols: Mists & Heaven

Life Cycle: the Elders

You can turn fate inside out. Gather and concentrate your insight.

What Can and Cannot Happen

- Rejoice in your family's harmony. It is a strong defense against attack.
- Your business affairs are going very well. They offer a wide range of possibilities to take over other enterprises. Gather and concentrate your creative energy.
- Plans for a significant relationship will go well if you make a real effort.
- You can expect a son in the near future.
- If you must go to court, have no fears. The spirits are with you.
- Don't worry about your health. If you fall ill, you will soon recover.

Advice to the Wayfarer

When you truly despair, always remember that the sun will follow the rain. Be true to the one who is true to you. If you hold to this friendship, you will find a way through. Don't let this tense situation shake your confidence in yourself. Though unforeseen events and sudden changes may occur, everything will work out to your advantage in the end. **Dharma**: the sudden flash of lightning reveals a brand new world.

• 12 Good and Evil

> Good and evil are divided by a very thin line.
> There is a noble spirit at the mountain gate
> And you will soon have good news from him.
> He will help you through your difficulties.

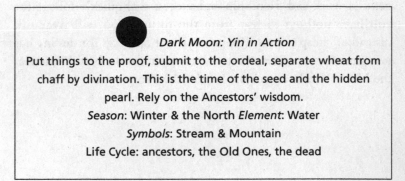

Dark Moon: Yin in Action
Put things to the proof, submit to the ordeal, separate wheat from chaff by divination. This is the time of the seed and the hidden pearl. Rely on the Ancestors' wisdom.
Season: Winter & the North *Element*: Water
Symbols: Stream & Mountain
Life Cycle: ancestors, the Old Ones, the dead

A time to discriminate clearly, for the noble one waits. Find the treasure hidden within you.

What Can and Cannot Happen

- Your household and family are in order. There are no changes to be made.
- Keep on as you are and your business will prosper. Selling assets should be put off, for it could create problems that you can't cope with. Find the hidden creative energy.
- Don't be afraid of a significant relationship. It is under a lucky star.
- If you want an heir, you will soon have one.
- You will receive news from a person you have not heard from for a long time.
- If you must go to court, the judgement will be in your favor.
- Don't change your home. You are settled and happy where you are.

• Be careful of your health. If you are sick, you won't recover until the fall.

Advice to the Wayfarer

Don't be impatient. Happiness follows unhappiness. You will soon have a new friend, but don't give up the old ones. Be more energetic in work and friendship and success will quickly follow, for you have nothing to fear from the future. You will wear silk instead of cheap cotton. Happiness is not far away, for destiny has it in store for you. Everything will turn out for the best. **Dharma**: the Noble Truths attract the love of the Protectors.

• 13 THE NOBLE SON

You belong to a noble family, rich and distinguished.
Once the Emperor has bestowed the Golden Girdle,
your name and fame will be in every mouth.
All the ways to the Golden Door are open to you.

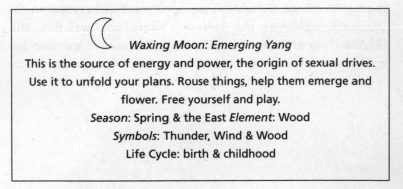

Waxing Moon: Emerging Yang
This is the source of energy and power, the origin of sexual drives.
Use it to unfold your plans. Rouse things, help them emerge and
flower. Free yourself and play.
Season: Spring & the East *Element*: Wood
Symbols: Thunder, Wind & Wood
Life Cycle: birth & childhood

*All is ready to burst forth and flower. Free yourself from the past and
find your true nature.*

What Can and Cannot Happen

- Your household is not in order. Work with patience and foresight to purify things and family joy will soon be restored.
- Business affairs are not too good at the moment, but you can
  count on making a considerable profit in the end. Fall and
  winter will bring great success. Put off important decisions
  until later. Creative energy is on the rise.
- A significant relationship will be successful. You have nothing
  to fear.
- If you are expecting a child, it will be a daughter.
- Friends coming from a distant place will run into difficulties,
  but you will be together in the end.
- Changing your home will bring you no advantage.

- If you are unwell, see a doctor as soon as possible to avoid lingering difficulties.

Advice to the Wayfarer

Don't rest on your laurels. You have lived through much in your life and now you must establish and support yourself. Don't worry about your family, though you shouldn't completely ignore them. With skill, diplomacy and endurance all will run smoothly. The Golden Door is open to you. It is in your power to step through it. **Dharma**: skillful means make you difficult to conquer.

• 14 THE SPIRIT CRANE

Like a spirit crane that leaves his cage,
you can fly wherever you choose.
North, South, East or West offer no obstacles.
Even the Ninth Paradise has opened its gates.

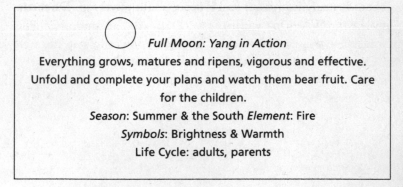

Full Moon: Yang in Action
Everything grows, matures and ripens, vigorous and effective.
Unfold and complete your plans and watch them bear fruit. Care
for the children.
Season: Summer & the South *Element*: Fire
Symbols: Brightness & Warmth
Life Cycle: adults, parents

The worlds of the spirit are open for you to enjoy.

What Can and Cannot Happen

- There is an enduring disharmony in your family. Search out the cause and resolve it. It wouldn't hurt to dedicate more time to family problems.
- Your business is very promising. Many opportunities offer themselves. Try to use all of them. Creative energy is at your service.
- If you want an heir, you will soon have one.
- If you are involved in litigation, don't go to court. Try to settle things in a friendly fashion.
- If your present living situation doesn't feel right and you can't see how it will improve, then plan to move. It can only be to your advantage.

Advice to the Wayfarer

The world is too much with you. People to see and things to do surround you. Give more attention to your friends. Have a long talk with your partner. You must overcome your restlessness and find the way back to yourself. Then you can do what you wish. Wander in peace and contentment, for all the ways are open. There is really no reason to be upset about anything. **Dharma**: invoke the Wise One within.

• 15 CATASTROPHE

A sudden catastrophe strikes.
Like a bird whose nest in the woods is destroyed,
you can only find protection
in a wild and hidden place.

Waning Moon: Emerging Yin
This is the time to harvest. It will bring insight as well as profit.
Reap and gather your crops. Conserve your energy and nourish the
spirits. Honor the experienced.
Season: Autumn & the West *Element*: Metal
Symbols: Mists & Heaven
Life Cycle: the Elders

---

*Hide. Stay calm and still. Come to rest again. Gather and concentrate
your insight. Fear nothing.*

What Can and Cannot Happen

- Your household is troubled and turbulent, but all will soon be back in balance even without your efforts.
- Business looks good. There are exceptional opportunities for an extraordinary success. Gather and concentrate creative energy.
- If there are problems in your significant relationship, they can be overcome.
- If you want an addition to the family, you will soon have a son.
- If you must go to court, the judgement will go in your favor.
- Your wish that a close friend be cured of his illness will soon be fulfilled.
- If you are planning a trip, you will reach your goal.

Advice to the Wayfarer

Hold back for now, but don't be discouraged. Don't force things even though you want immediate change. Set to work methodically with your eye on the goal and success will soon be yours. Forget about the nasty things people say. They are meaningless and can't affect your future. Be tactful and careful with the opposite sex. At first, all you encounter will be trouble and affliction, but in the end you will overcome everything. Someone wishes you evil, but soon all that sorrow will be behind you. For now, accept your fate with patience. Don't be worried! **Dharma**: we only learn through suffering intelligently.

• 16 A HAPPY FACE

A long anxious face is not the thing now.
Forget your cares and enjoy what life offers you.
A workman's capable hands
clear away the dust that hides a precious jade.

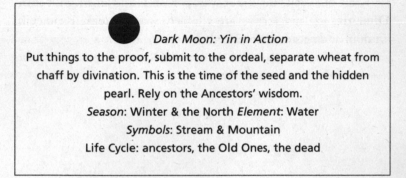

Dark Moon: Yin in Action
Put things to the proof, submit to the ordeal, separate wheat from
chaff by divination. This is the time of the seed and the hidden
pearl. Rely on the Ancestors' wisdom.
Season: Winter & the North *Element*: Water
Symbols: Stream & Mountain
Life Cycle: ancestors, the Old Ones, the dead

When you have found the hidden treasure, why should you be sad?

What Can and Cannot Happen

- Your household enjoys an enviable harmony that will last. You
  will benefit from it particularly in fall and winter.
- Count on an extraordinary success in business and a considerable increase in profits. Find the hidden creative energy.
- Plans for a significant relationship will flourish. You will soon
  be united with the one you love.
- Don't go to court, for the chances are against you. Settle out of
  court in a friendly fashion.
- Don't change your home. Your present place has all you need.
- If you are unwell, go to a doctor. A carelessly handled illness
  could be very wearisome now.

Advice to the Wayfarer

This is a lucky time. All is harmonious and you can concentrate on your plans. Don't be thoughtless and try to do too much. You could easily lose your way. Be methodical. Bring yin and yang into harmony and your plans will fulfill themselves. Your inner balance will attract friends. Save something from your good fortune to repay an old debt, for a virtuous person is rewarded with luck. **Dharma**: joy and sorrow are a closely woven cloak. Rejoice in wisdom and accept suffering gladly.

• 17 TURN A DEAF EAR

> Turn a deaf ear to scandal and gossip.
> When you believe lies and deceptive words,
> it is as if you tried to still your hunger
> by eating the picture of a cake.

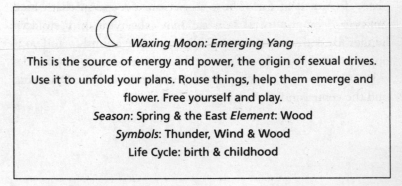

Waxing Moon: Emerging Yang

This is the source of energy and power, the origin of sexual drives.
Use it to unfold your plans. Rouse things, help them emerge and
flower. Free yourself and play.
Season: Spring & the East *Element*: Wood
Symbols: Thunder, Wind & Wood
Life Cycle: birth & childhood

If you can free yourself of illusions, envy and greed, this will be a very fertile and creative time.

What Can and Cannot Happen

- Your family is very turbulent now, so concentrate on making it better.
- You have a clear field in business. Don't let trivial obstacles bother you. Creative energy is on the rise.
- Your relationship is troubled, but a heart-to-heart talk will clear things up.
- If you are expecting a child, the birth will be uncomplicated.
- If you are caught in legal struggles, don't be unyielding. A friendly reconciliation is better than going to court.
- Don't change your home, even if you feel uncomfortable. You would soon find yourself in a very difficult situation.

- Don't worry about your illness. If you are patient, it will soon be cured.

Advice to the Wayfarer

Once you are caught in the whirlpool of scandal and gossip, you will be dragged deeper and deeper until you forget your own plans. Turn a deaf ear! These stories are deception that breed vanity and emptiness. If you eat that cake, you only swallow hunger. Be realistic about your family, your relationship and your opportunities. Don't be influenced by outside advisors. Don't take risks unless you are convinced that the plan is feasible. **Dharma**: find the center and stay on the way.

• 18 THE CROW AND THE RABBIT

The crow sinks below the horizon as the rabbit rises,
symbols of sun and moon.
Since the beginning of the world, day and night have alternated.
Sages see it as an image of the changes in our lives.

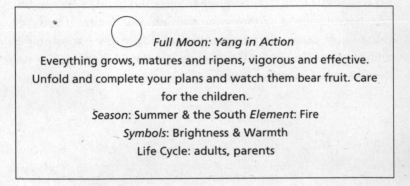

Full Moon: Yang in Action
Everything grows, matures and ripens, vigorous and effective.
Unfold and complete your plans and watch them bear fruit. Care
for the children.
Season: Summer & the South *Element*: Fire
Symbols: Brightness & Warmth
Life Cycle: adults, parents

*Everything is coming to fruition now. Put yourself in order, find the
inner balance, and take advantage of the time.*

What Can and Cannot Happen

- Have no cares about your household. Everything is harmonious
and in order.
- Your business is running itself. The signs are good that there
will be a real increase in profits in the near future. Creative
energy is at your service.
- If you wish a significant relationship, you will soon find a suitable partner.
- If you must go to court, have no fears. The judgement will be
in your favor.
- If you have lost something precious, have patience. It will soon
be found.

- If you are sick, see a doctor as soon as possible to avoid complications.

Advice to the Wayfarer

This is the time to put your house in order. You have let things slide. Above all, clear up confused relationships. Don't waste time, get to work! This is not the place to relax. Harmony between sun and moon is a good sign for your goal and your destiny. If you cultivate inner peace and satisfaction with life, many opportunities will open to you. Everything is possible now. **Dharma**: use the keen sword of discrimination!

• 19 STORMY SEAS

A ferry returns, tossing and turning in the deep valleys
of a storm.
We can't call this stable or calm!
The steersman can do nothing.
His boat careens without a guide.

)) *Waning Moon: Emerging Yin*

This is the time to harvest. It will bring insight as well as profit.
Reap and gather your crops. Conserve your energy and nourish the
spirits. Honor the experienced.

Season: Autumn & the West *Element*: Metal

Symbols: Mists & Heaven

Life Cycle: the Elders

---

*Feeling yourself a passive victim, you are sucked into the downward
spiral. Come to your senses! The crop is ready to harvest.*

What Can and Cannot Happen

- There are problems in your household you haven't been able to
solve. Try again with all your energy so they won't get worse.
- Your business isn't going to run itself. You must work at it to
reap the rewards. Don't think you will make a fortune overnight. Gather and concentrate creative energy.
- Your relationship has foundered, but it is out of your hands for
now. Be patient and contain yourself.
- You won't have children at a time like this.
- Don't change your home. In this insecure situation, it would
only work against you.
- Be careful of sickness, for it could prove very wearisome.

Advice to the Wayfarer

At the moment you are at sea in an unenviable situation and it is affecting your self-confidence. You need courage and endurance. Collect your energy and you can reach the shore that beckons. Release yourself from all that worries or hinders you. Take hold of your future with both hands. Your time will come! Grasp the opportunity with both hands and use everything that is available. **Dharma**: the greedy person is blown by the winds of desire. Take thought!

• 20 AFTER THE RAIN

> After a long rain, we joyously watch the heavens clear.
> The sun and moon grow slowly brighter.
> The gloomy days are over, so be happy and joyous.
> You will bound through the Dragon Door in one leap.

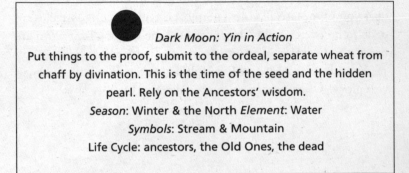

Dark Moon: Yin in Action
Put things to the proof, submit to the ordeal, separate wheat from chaff by divination. This is the time of the seed and the hidden pearl. Rely on the Ancestors' wisdom.
Season: Winter & the North *Element*: Water
Symbols: Stream & Mountain
Life Cycle: ancestors, the Old Ones, the dead

You have found the hidden treasure. Open the spirit world and enjoy its riches.

What Can and Cannot Happen

- Your household is in order. There is nothing to worry about except keeping your inner strength.
- Business transactions are not promising, so hold back. You can't count on success now. Be patient. Find the hidden creative energy.
- Your relationship depends on you right now. Your partner's reluctance is really meaningless.
- If you are expecting a child, it will be a daughter.
- If you have conflicts, don't go to court. The judgement will go against you. Try to settle the matter in a friendly fashion.
- If you have lost something, look for it diligently and you will find it.

- If you don't feel well, don't try to cure yourself. Go to a doctor, who will cure you quickly and easily.

Advice to the Wayfarer

Why do you drag your unhappy past around? All that is over and done with. Be happy, like someone who wakes out of a terrible nightmare and finds it wasn't true after all. You must work hard for what you want. Use all your energy and endurance. 'Obstacles are made to be overcome' is the motto for the coming time. You are under a god's protection and no one can harm you wherever you are. Your deepest wishes will be fulfilled and you will be crowned with glory! **Dharma**: greet the Awakening One!

• 21 THE UNION OF SUN AND MOON

Blessed is the union of man and woman
married in the joining of yin and yang.
This pair will know a sweet dream of happiness.
The harmony of Sun and Moon is the sign of fulfillment.

Waxing Moon: Emerging Yang
This is the source of energy and power, the origin of sexual drives.
Use it to unfold your plans. Rouse things, help them emerge and
flower. Free yourself and play.
Season: Spring & the East *Element*: Wood
Symbols: Thunder, Wind & Wood
Life Cycle: birth & childhood

---

*This union is truly blessed and unfolds a brand new spring. Be happy
and be free of the sorrows of the past!*

What Can and Cannot Happen

- Your household is harmonious and you can be proud and happy.
- You will have no trouble running your business. The signs point to success and a considerable growth in profits. Creative energy is on the rise.
- A significant relationship will bring all you wish and this happiness will last.
- If you are expecting a child, it will be a son.
- If you must go to court, the judge will rule in your favor.
- Though your present situation answers your needs, a change of home might prove even better.
- If you are sick, don't worry. But don't take things too lightly.

Advice to the Wayfarer

This is a happy time and everything will go as you wish, but don't be too confident. Even when the stars are favorable, you can't take everything for granted. The world doesn't owe you a living. You have to work at it. **Dharma**: gather the light and Paradise will open.

● 22 TIMELY RAIN

Young rice sprouts wither and fade in the drought.
Heaven be thanked for the timely rain,
worth a thousand pieces of gold!
If you are in difficulties, someone will help you.

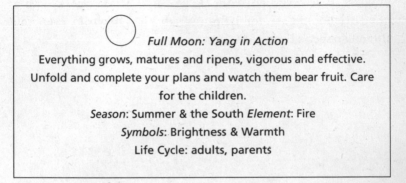

Full Moon: Yang in Action
Everything grows, matures and ripens, vigorous and effective.
Unfold and complete your plans and watch them bear fruit. Care
for the children.
Season: Summer & the South *Element*: Fire
Symbols: Brightness & Warmth
Life Cycle: adults, parents

*Thank Heaven for these kind words as you watch your world ripen and
your hopes bear fruit.*

What Can and Cannot Happen

- Nothing can disturb the peace of your household. Try to keep it that way!
- There is a very good chance of extraordinary profits in business. Be patient. Success will come later rather than sooner. Creative energy is at your service.
- If you want a significant relationship, don't delay. This union is destined for happiness.
- Don't go to court, for the judgement will go against you. Try reconciliation with your opponent.
- Don't change your home now, it will bring absolutely no advantage.

• Take care of your health. Have a thorough examination, for a hidden disorder could break out and cause considerable trouble.

Advice to the Wayfarer

At the moment, positive and negative are balanced in your situation. Take stock of things and draw conclusions about your further progress. Before you put your designs into action, speak with a good friend and ask for help and advice. **Dharma**: even the Buddha respects the right time.

• 23 THE HEAVENLY DOOR IS CLOSED

How sad! The Heavenly Door is closed.
You can't land on the moon and climb the fairy Laurel Tree.
But a powerful Protector from on high
Will soon help you in your difficulties.

)) *Waning Moon: Emerging Yin*

This is the time to harvest. It will bring insight as well as profit.
Reap and gather your crops. Conserve your energy and nourish the
spirits. Honor the experienced.

Season: Autumn & the West *Element*: Metal

Symbols: Mists & Heaven

Life Cycle: the Elders

Gather and concentrate your insight and the Helpers will soon arrive.

What Can and Cannot Happen

- At the moment your household is in trouble. This is a tense situation and you should avoid doing anything that will make it tenser.
- Business plans materialize slowly. Negotiations are sticky. Don't be discouraged, be determined! Gather and concentrate creative energy.
- Your desire for a significant relationship won't work out now, but don't lose hope. It is postponed, not canceled.
- Be careful on trips, particularly in traffic, and there will be no accidents.
- Don't go before a judge, for the chances are against you. Seek a compromise out of court.
- Changing your home will only bring more difficulties.

- If you are ill, take your illness seriously and see a doctor immediately.

Advice to the Wayfarer

You are held back by family and household difficulties. You must restore peace as soon as possible. You can expect good news soon. People are willing to help you with your problems and your partner is ready to meet you halfway. Work at it. Don't insist on your so-called rights and all your difficulties will vanish. Stay calm and be cautious. That is all that is asked of you now. **Dharma**: invoke the Great Protectors and have compassion for your fellow humans.

• 24 A Household in Danger

> Your household is in danger of falling apart
> through unjust mutual recriminations.
> It is like sadly wilting flowers
> that fall into the boundless salt sea.

Dark Moon: Yin in Action

Put things to the proof, submit to the ordeal, separate wheat from chaff by divination. This is the time of the seed and the hidden pearl. Rely on the Ancestors' wisdom.

Season: Winter & the North *Element*: Water
Symbols: Stream & Mountain
Life Cycle: ancestors, the Old Ones, the dead

You are caught in a downward spiral of anger and greed. Wake up, Noble One! Find the treasure hidden within.

What Can and Cannot Happen

- Your family relations are troubled and will remain so for quite a while. Avoid confrontations at all costs. Actively seek reconciliation.
- In business you confront a mountain of obstacles. You simply can't count on success for now. Find the hidden creative energy.
- If you want a significant relationship, be very patient. Your plans will take a long time to work out.
- At all costs, don't go to court. The judgement will surely go against you.
- If you feel unwell, see a doctor. Being remiss about this could cause a long and wearisome illness.

Advice to the Wayfarer

Above all, you must be patient. You must put up with a lot. Beware of scandal and gossip. Do everything very carefully. Be honest, scrupulous and friendly and you will see things suddenly change. If you want to change your home, do it without a second thought. A new place will make things much easier to deal with. **Dharma**: exercise compassion and insight for your fellow creatures.

• 25 THE OLD, DRY SPRING

Like an old, dry spring that fills with fresh water,
joy bubbles forth once more.
All your sorrow and misfortune
now belong to the past.

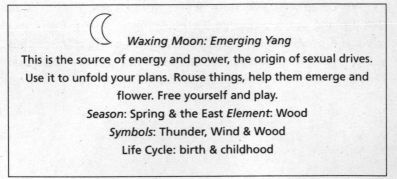

Waxing Moon: Emerging Yang
This is the source of energy and power, the origin of sexual drives.
Use it to unfold your plans. Rouse things, help them emerge and
flower. Free yourself and play.
Season: Spring & the East *Element*: Wood
Symbols: Thunder, Wind & Wood
Life Cycle: birth & childhood

*A new birth of spirit and joy. The sorrows of the past are illusions. Let
them go and the world will flower!*

What Can and Cannot Happen

- Your household is harmonious and there is no sign that it will change.
- Developing your business will involve difficulties, but don't be discouraged. Creative energy is on the rise.
- If you want a significant relationship, talk to your friend very soon. This union is destined to be happy.
- If you are going on a trip, plan very carefully or you will find yourself caught up in difficulties.
- Don't change your home now. You are comfortably settled where you are.
- If you are sick, be careful. Recovery won't be so easy.

Advice to the Wayfarer

You have lived through a lot in the recent past and you are a bit despondent. But the situation won't change while you keep your hands in your pockets and do nothing but mope. Make sure your chief and your friends know of your ability, which is not the case at the moment. Once you are recognized, your career will unfold to your complete satisfaction. Set to work patiently, and realize that nothing can be achieved by force. Impatience is a very bad advisor. A benevolent and highly placed person will come to your aid, for you please him or her in everything you do. **Dharma**: change your heart and you change your life.

• 26 SPREADING RUMORS

Rumors are spreading
that an embassy from Heaven will soon appear
to confer honor and rank on all.
Sadly, the rumors prove to be false.

◯ *Full Moon: Yang in Action*

**Everything grows, matures and ripens, vigorous and effective.
Unfold and complete your plans and watch them bear fruit. Care
for the children.**

Season: Summer & the South *Element*: Fire

Symbols: Brightness & Warmth

Life Cycle: adults, parents

---

*If you can free yourself from the greedy desire for fame and power, this
can be a very fertile time.*

What Can and Cannot Happen

- Your household is in disorder. Work hard to prevent the outbreak of strife.
- Though business affairs will be unsuccessful now, and you can expect no immediate increase in income, creative energy is at your service.
- Don't begin a significant relationship. This is not the right partner for you.
- If you are expecting a child, it will be a daughter.
- Don't go to court, for the judgement will go against you.
- Don't change your home. You have a good base where you are, so make use of all the chances it offers.

Advice to the Wayfarer

Be realistic and practical in your philosophy of life. Don't strive for fame and fortune. Hold back and wait until your time comes. Don't promise anything rashly, for you can be sure all your promises will have to be kept. Be constant and strong in all you do. **Dharma**: use the keen sword of discrimination to separate illusion from desire.

• 27 STRONG FENCES

Strong fences
make a secure and joyous home.
A life without dangers
awaits you.

) *Waning Moon: Emerging Yin*

This is the time to harvest. It will bring insight as well as profit.
Reap and gather your crops. Conserve your energy and nourish the
spirits. Honor the experienced.

Season: Autumn & the West *Element*: Metal

Symbols: Mists & Heaven

Life Cycle: the Elders

---

*Live within the strong guard of your accumulated insight and enjoy the
rich harvest of your life.*

What Can and Cannot Happen

- Your household is in perfect order. Enjoy its warmth and security.
- There are business obstacles, but you can overcome them.
  Expect great profits in the near future. Gather and concentrate
  creative energy.
- This is not the time to begin a significant relationship. It will
  only lead to difficulties.
- If you are expecting a child, it will be a daughter.
- If you must go to court, the judgement will be in your favor.
- If you are thinking of changing your home, go through with
  your plans. They will only bring you gain.
- Be careful of your health! An illness now could last a long
  time.

Advice to the Wayfarer

You are full of plans that remain undeveloped because of the way
you always delay things. You give yourself unnecessary worries
that sap your strength. A good friend is offering help now and you
should by all means take it. This influence can help you carry out
your plans. **Dharma**: dwell in the truth of your insight into illusion.

• 28 CLOUD COVERS THE RISING MOON

Majestic and graceful, the moon rises in the west.
If something hides it, it is still there, crescent or full, waxing or
waning.
A cloud covers the moon now and your situation looks dim.
The clouds will soon disperse and the friendly light shine.

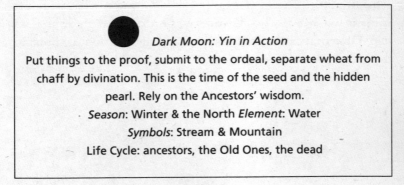

Dark Moon: Yin in Action
Put things to the proof, submit to the ordeal, separate wheat from
chaff by divination. This is the time of the seed and the hidden
pearl. Rely on the Ancestors' wisdom.
Season: Winter & the North *Element*: Water
Symbols: Stream & Mountain
Life Cycle: ancestors, the Old Ones, the dead

*Find the treasure of joy, insight and compassion hidden in the chaff
of life.*

What Can and Cannot Happen

- Your family situation seems tense and upset, but don't take it
  too seriously. These conflicts aren't deep and joy will soon be
  restored.
- Business prospects are very good, but there are many obstacles
  to overcome before success is yours. Find the hidden creative
  energy.
- Plan your trip very carefully and you won't be caught in difficulties.
- Your significant relationship with your partner is disturbed.
- If you are expecting a child, beware of complications.
- Don't go to court. The judgement will go against you.

- Don't change your home. Where you are now is the best place for you.
- If you are sick, seek help immediately. Your disorder can be quickly cured.

Advice to the Wayfarer

You think you are looking at a mountain of difficulties, but it is actually a little hill you can easily climb. Gossip is what will hurt you, so watch every word you say. Carefully weigh your next step. **Dharma**: call to the Protector and she will appear, holding the gift of compassion.

• 29 THE HOLY SWORD

The holy sword gleams and glances,
unsullied by dirt or grime.
In the hand of a worthy man,
this gallantry rouses both wonder and envy.

Waxing Moon: Emerging Yang

This is the source of energy and power, the origin of sexual drives.
Use it to unfold your plans. Rouse things, help them emerge and
flower. Free yourself and play.

Season: Spring & the East *Element*: Wood

Symbols: Thunder, Wind & Wood

Life Cycle: birth & childhood

---

*Be incisive and aggressive in the battle for the way of love and the world
will flower around you.*

What Can and Cannot Happen

- Your household is tense and disturbed. Act now and the peace of your family won't be destroyed. Be balanced and majestic.
- Business affairs are going very well. Be adroit and cautious and you will make a considerable profit. Creative energy is on the rise.
- Go through with your plans for a significant relationship. This union will be very happy.
- If you are expecting a child, it will be a daughter.
- Your guests will arrive sooner than you expect.
- Don't go to court. Settle peacefully through a compromise.
- If you are sick, go to a doctor. He will quickly cure you.

Advice to the Wayfarer

Because you are alone and must make decisions alone, you are often discouraged and disheartened. You don't want to confront these choices. Clarify all your relationships, private and public. Don't hesitate to ask a good friend or an authority for advice. Above all, beware of false friends. When the holy sword is drawn from its sheath, it will spread honor and splendor for miles around. **Dharma**: cut through spiritual materialism!

• 30 SNAKE IN THE GRASS

A white stork hides an arrow under its feathers
so that it can shoot at you!
Looking for brushwood in the high grass, you encounter a snake
whose bite could seriously harm you.

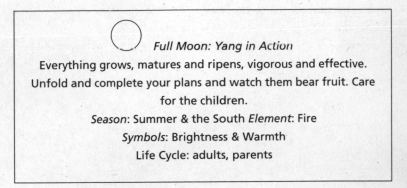

Full Moon: Yang in Action
Everything grows, matures and ripens, vigorous and effective.
Unfold and complete your plans and watch them bear fruit. Care
for the children.
Season: Summer & the South *Element*: Fire
Symbols: Brightness & Warmth
Life Cycle: adults, parents

*An enemy is hidden in all this abundance. Is it your neighbor? Or is it
your Old Greedy Self?*

What Can and Cannot Happen

- Your family and household are in order. Between your four walls you have no cares.
- Business is exhausting now, and there is no immediate chance of profits. Don't worry! Your time will come. Be patient and careful in all you do and you won't come to harm. Creative energy is at your service.
- Your plans for a significant relationship won't succeed. Be very careful. Don't expose yourself to danger.
- If you plan to change your home, put it off until later. Right now, it would not work to your advantage.

Advice to the Wayfarer

Be as closed as an oyster, careful and honest in everything you say and do. Don't get entangled through duplicity. Anything you do that goes against your conscience and ideals will certainly work to your disadvantage. Don't aim too high, rather, take precaution against all possible unpleasantness. **Dharma**: renounce greedy ambitions and return to the way.

• 31 ADVICE FROM A GOOD SPIRIT

You life unfolds enjoyably and comfortably.
Drink a cup of fine tea after dinner!
You are protected from sorrow and poverty.
Perhaps a good spirit will bestow her valuable advice on you!

Waning Moon: Emerging Yin
This is the time to harvest. It will bring insight as well as profit.
Reap and gather your crops. Conserve your energy and nourish the
spirits. Honor the experienced.
Season: Autumn & the West *Element*: Metal
Symbols: Mists & Heaven
Life Cycle: the Elders

Enjoy the fruits of a well-spent life in the joys of the imagination.

What Can and Cannot Happen

- Your family is very turbulent, swirling with hidden tensions. Remedy the situation as soon as possible so peace can reign again.
- Be patient in your business dealings, consistent but not inconsiderate. Gather and concentrate creative energy.
- If you want a significant relationship, everything will unfold happily.
- If you are expecting a child, it will be a daughter.
- If you are waiting for guests, they will soon arrive.
- If you want to change your home, it will turn out much to your advantage.
- If you are sick, see a doctor immediately to avoid a tedious convalescence.

Advice to the Wayfarer

You have nothing to fear for the future. Be patient. All will go joyously without you taking any special care. But don't just sit there with your hands in your pockets. Be happy with what is given you to do. If you want something, you must be active. Be calm even when you encounter difficulties. **Dharma**: Listen to the still small voice. Then act on it!

• 32 HIDDEN IN THE STONE

How long your journey seems and how dark your future,
    For no one sees the jade hidden in the stone.
    One day a clever stonecutter will saw it out,
    and a priceless jewel will see the light of day.

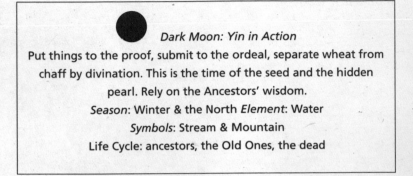

Dark Moon: Yin in Action

Put things to the proof, submit to the ordeal, separate wheat from chaff by divination. This is the time of the seed and the hidden pearl. Rely on the Ancestors' wisdom.

Season: Winter & the North *Element*: Water

Symbols: Stream & Mountain

Life Cycle: ancestors, the Old Ones, the dead

How long it seems when you journey to find yourself. But one day, the precious pearl appears in your heart!

What Can and Cannot Happen

- Your household and family are in good order. Everyone is healthy and happy. Be pleased with your luck.
- You confront a mountain of difficulties in business, but you can count on success. Don't despair! Find the hidden creative energy.
- If you wish to begin a significant relationship, chances are good that it will be happy.
- No children at the moment. Perhaps a doctor can help you.
- If you expect guests, they will be late. Be patient!
- Don't go to court, for the judgement will go against you. You have a good chance in an out-of-court settlement.
- If you want to travel, think carefully about where you want to go.

Advice to the Wayfarer

You can't tell what is hidden inside a stone, so you must find a wise person to lay it bare. In other words, if you can't solve your problems yourself, get someone you trust to advise you. There is a lot in your future that you can't see at the moment. Be very careful in all you do. **Dharma**: skillful means produce far-reaching results.

• 33 THE IDIOT'S JEWEL

Only an idiot
would frantically search the world for his precious jewel
when he had hidden it
in a pile of rocks near home.

Waxing Moon: Emerging Yang

This is the source of energy and power, the origin of sexual drives.
Use it to unfold your plans. Rouse things, help them emerge and
flower. Free yourself and play.
Season: Spring & the East *Element*: Wood
Symbols: Thunder, Wind & Wood
Life Cycle: birth & childhood

---

*Why climb the distant, barren mountains when the spring is bursting
out all around you?*

What Can and Cannot Happen

- Your home and family are in perfect order. Expect a happy future.
- You must be patient in business matters. Success will definitely
  come one day, so don't worry about it. Creative energy is rising.
- Your plans for a significant relationship will be successful.
- If you are expecting a child, it will be a son.
- If you are planning a trip, be very careful. There are obstacles
  that may prevent you from reaching your destination.
- If you are involved in litigation, don't go to court. The judge-
  ment will go against you.
- This is not the time to change your home! Think any move
  over very carefully and seek expert advice.
- You don't have to worry about your health, but do be careful.

Advice to the Wayfarer

You can't see the forest for the trees at the moment. You are looking for things far away when they are right in front of your face. Open your eyes and look around. You will soon find what you are looking for. **Dharma**: distance yourself from the compulsive desire to seek fame and fortune.

• 34 THE CLOUDLESS SKY

The sun is shining on you,
bright and clear
in a cloudless sky.
Everything is going as you wish.

○ *Full Moon: Yang in Action*

Everything grows, matures and ripens, vigorous and effective.
Unfold and complete your plans and watch them bear fruit. Care
for the children.

Season: Summer & the South *Element*: Fire
Symbols: Brightness & Warmth
Life Cycle: adults, parents

Your heart is clear and the way is open. The ripe fruit falls into
your hand.

What Can and Cannot Happen

- Your household is peaceful and stable. Everything is running without problems.
- You have planned the sale of a large business. Think again. Is this the right plan? It could cause problems that would eat up your success.
- There are no obstacles to a significant relationship. Go through with your plans. The union will be happy.
- If you are expecting a child, be under a doctor's care to avoid complications.
- Plan your trip well so you will avoid being caught in unforeseen difficulties.
- Don't go to court, for the judgement will go against you.

- Don't change your home. The place you are now offers a very good future.
- If you are feeling unwell, take care or you may become truly ill.

Advice to the Wayfarer

This is a peaceful period, but it is time to gather your forces and do something significant. Be honorable and sincere in your conduct. This is not the time to plague yourself with doubts and cares, for everything will go as you wish. You can hope for a very bright future! **Dharma**: Make your heart transparent. Transform your dark desires.

• 35 THE WELL-LIT STREET

A well-lit street
stretches out before you,
where once there were thistles
and thorns.

> ☽ *Waning Moon: Emerging Yin*
> This is the time to harvest. It will bring insight as well as profit.
> Reap and gather your crops. Conserve your energy and nourish the
> spirits. Honor the experienced.
> *Season*: Autumn & the West *Element*: Metal
> *Symbols*: Mists & Heaven
> Life Cycle: the Elders

If you concentrate your insight, what you once thought painful will turn to light.

What Can and Cannot Happen

- You household and family are at odds with each other. You must root out the problems and restore harmony.
- Your business possibilities are outstanding. You will soon be successful and earn extraordinary profits. Gather and concentrate creative energy.
- If you want to begin a significant relationship, don't be daunted by obstacles. A heart-to-heart talk with your friend will soon dissolve them.
- If you are expecting a child, don't worry about complications. If you are nervous, a doctor will soon calm your fears.
- If you must go to court, don't worry. The judgement will be in your favor.

- If you want to change your home or homeland, go through with your plans. Everything will turn out to your advantage.
- If you feel unwell, see a doctor. You will be cured of a hidden illness.

Advice to the Wayfarer

Your family's reputation has suffered, and you must work hard to rebuild it. Taking a trip now would be totally irresponsible, so give up the idea. Have no doubts or cares, for your lucky day will come. You must overcome old difficulties and suffering before your wishes come true. **Dharma**: let the smile of the Goddess transform your sorrowing heart.

● 36 Monkey on a Golden Chain

The mighty, clever Monkey has been imprisoned.
He throws off his golden chains
and returns to his mountain home,
joyous and free once more.

Dark Moon: Yin in Action

Put things to the proof, submit to the ordeal, separate wheat from
chaff by divination. This is the time of the seed and the hidden
pearl. Rely on the Ancestors' wisdom.
Season: Winter & the North *Element*: Water
Symbols: Stream & Mountain
Life Cycle: ancestors, the Old Ones, the dead

---

*Freed at last from chains of greed, you return to the wild freedom of
the heart.*

What Can and Cannot Happen

- There is confusion in your family now, but it will pass. Have no fears.
- You can expect considerable business success, but the time is not ripe yet. You must patiently wait a while longer. Find the hidden creative energy.
- Don't rush into a significant relationship. Spend enough time with your prospective partner to get to know them. Then you won't be disappointed later.
- The guests you are waiting for will arrive any moment.
- If you are expecting a child, take very good care of yourself. Put yourself under a doctor's care.

- Even though you are in the right in a legal matter, don't be too eager to insist on it. Wouldn't you rather keep your partner's friendship?
- If you can, change your home now. All the signs are in your favor.

Advice to the Wayfarer

You really are too impatient! You want everything done now and thus leave fate nowhere to work. Don't be so irritated and contentious. Avoid strife at all costs, for it will only bring you sorrow and you will deeply regret it. Free yourself from all ties. Don't put yourself under pressure, but let things come of themselves. Set to work only when you see a real opportunity. The road to success is wide open. It only depends on you to walk on it. **Dharma**: does Monkey have a Buddha-nature? Oh my, yes!

● 37 THE BURNING CANDLE

A burning candle flickers
and throws an unsteady light.
Do not expose yourself to danger.
Live hidden in retreat.

Waxing Moon: Emerging Yang
This is the source of energy and power, the origin of sexual drives.
Use it to unfold your plans. Rouse things, help them emerge and
flower. Free yourself and play.
Season: Spring & the East *Element*: Wood
Symbols: Thunder, Wind & Wood
Life Cycle: birth & childhood

*You are full of creative energy, but you must keep it hidden. There are
enemies all around you.*

What Can and Cannot Happen

- Your family and household are in order, so don't try to fix them.
- Business seems very difficult, but if you work cautiously and methodically you can make a considerable profit. Creative energy is on the rise.
- If you expect a child, seek a doctor's help. There may be complications.
- If you must go to court, don't worry. The result will be a peaceful reconciliation. So why not try to affect a settlement out of court?
- The guests you are waiting for will soon call to say when they are coming.

- Don't change your home. You would find it very hard to live in a new place.
- If you are ill, you will soon recover.

Advice to the Wayfarer

Your situation is not enviable, primarily because you are not clear about which direction you should take. Pull back and think your next step over in peace. Then all will go well. If you take a wrong turn, it could seriously harm you. **Dharma**: seek the source of your illusions.

• 38 THE BOOK OF WISDOM

You hope that the book of heavenly wisdom
will fall from the moonlit heavens and drop into your hand.
Lowering clouds and driving rain darken the skies,
so you will have to wait until the storm is over.

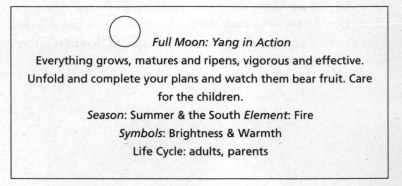

Full Moon: Yang in Action
Everything grows, matures and ripens, vigorous and effective.
Unfold and complete your plans and watch them bear fruit. Care
for the children.
Season: Summer & the South *Element*: Fire
Symbols: Brightness & Warmth
Life Cycle: adults, parents

*As you wait out this sudden storm, the fruits of wisdom can ripen
within you.*

What Can and Cannot Happen

- Your family is full of worry and care about the health of its members. Stay calm and you can restore peace and happiness.
- Watch and wait in business. Your time has not yet come. It would be very difficult to increase profits at the moment. Creative energy is at your service.
- Don't seek a significant relationship now, for your efforts would be unsuccessful.
- If you must go to court, count on a satisfactory agreement as the outcome.
- If you aren't attached to your home, a change will be to your advantage.

- If you are ill, by all means consult a doctor. This illness could prove serious.

Advice to the Wayfarer

Don't chase dreams and fantasies, work with the facts at hand. Don't wait for someone to give you everything on a silver platter. Be active and energetic. Try to attain your goal now, for your dissatisfaction comes from your apathy. Be very careful in traffic and help older family members to cross the street. **Dharma**: resolution is the key to the heavens.

• 39 Beyond the Horizon

> News reaches you from beyond the horizon,
> as mysterious, ridiculous and nonsensical as a man polishing a
> rock into a mirror.
> If you don't concern yourself, you will be spared a lot of trouble.

Waning Moon: Emerging Yin
This is the time to harvest. It will bring insight as well as profit.
Reap and gather your crops. Conserve your energy and nourish the
spirits. Honor the experienced.
Season: Autumn & the West *Element*: Metal
Symbols: Mists & Heaven
Life Cycle: the Elders

Use your concentrated insight to cut through this fog of silly illusions.

What Can and Cannot Happen

- Your household is in order, even if there are small differences in the family.
- Be careful now. There is real danger of an accident.
- Business is difficult, but if you carefully follow the course of things you will find a real opportunity for success. Gather and concentrate creative energy.
- A significant relationship isn't possible now. Your current partner is not right.
- If you are expecting a child, it will be a daughter.
- The guests you are expecting are already on their way.

- Think twice about going to court. The signs for success are not good.
- If you are ill, the recovery will be slow but complete.

Advice to the Wayfarer

Don't get so upset about things. At the moment, you simply don't know where to start. You can see no clear path ahead of you. The great danger is that you will draw the wrong conclusions. Let friends advise you on important decisions. It is not true that good advice is expensive. Be careful in traffic and in sports activities. **Dharma**: beware the right tool in the wrong hands. Use the keen sword of discrimination.

● 40 THE RISING MOON

The sun sets
and the moon rises,
gaining power from the sun.
This is the time of the woman and the yin.

Dark Moon: Yin in Action

Put things to the proof, submit to the ordeal, separate wheat from chaff by divination. This is the time of the seed and the hidden pearl. Rely on the Ancestors' wisdom.

Season: Winter & the North *Element*: Water

Symbols: Stream & Mountain

Life Cycle: ancestors, the Old Ones, the dead

Know the male, but act as the female. That is the hidden wisdom of the way.

What Can and Cannot Happen

- Your household is on unfriendly terms at the moment. Women in particular should be careful not extend their influence too far. Harmony comes from mutual respect and attention. No one should seek to rule.

- Your business is not too prosperous. Be patient, for it will take quite a while before success comes. Find the hidden creative energy.

- Plans for a significant relationship will probably not be successful.

- Don't go to court, for the judgement will go against you. If you have lost something you care about, you will probably not find it again.

- Have no cares about your health. If you fall ill, you will soon recover.

Advice to the Wayfarer

Personal problems are in the foreground now, and it will take much tact and patience to find a lasting solution. Look for the fundamental cause of the problem and root the evil out. Take time for a real discussion, but don't get emotionally overwrought. **Dharma**: if you keep a green bough in your heart, the singing bird will come.

• 41 HONEY-SWEET WORDS

Beware of words sweet as honey that betray your love and care.
You once treated a thief like your own son.
You would be humiliated and endangered
if you fall into the same trap again.

Waxing Moon: Emerging Yang

This is the source of energy and power, the origin of sexual drives.
Use it to unfold your plans. Rouse things, help them emerge and
flower. Free yourself and play.

Season: Spring & the East *Element*: Wood
Symbols: Thunder, Wind & Wood
Life Cycle: birth & childhood

---

*If you can free yourself from this web of sweet poisoned words, this can
be a very fertile time.*

What Can and Cannot Happen

- Your household is in order, but it could change in a moment.
  Watch for the signs and act quickly to avoid misunderstandings.
- If you want a significant relationship, be patient. It will take
  time.
- If you want an heir, you will soon have one.
- Settle conflicts out of court by finding an arbitrator.
- This is not a good time to change your home. If you must, be
  very careful!
- Be careful of your health, but don't worry. Any sickness will
  soon be healed.

Advice to the Wayfarer

Don't be ruled by your emotions. Be realistic about evaluating your surroundings. If you take this advice to heart, you won't be a victim again. **Dharma**: stand firm against the Queen of Illusions.

• 42 THE EARTHLY PARADISE

> You are showered
> with heavenly gifts
> and live in an earthly paradise,
> whether you realize it or not.

◯ *Full Moon: Yang in Action*

**Everything grows, matures and ripens, vigorous and effective.
Unfold and complete your plans and watch them bear fruit. Care
for the children.**

Season: Summer & the South *Element*: Fire

Symbols: Brightness & Warmth

Life Cycle: adults, parents

Look around you, Noble One. Open your eyes and you are in paradise.

What Can and Cannot Happen

- Your household and family are in good order. You can count on the fact that nothing will change.
- Your business is very promising. You could make a considerable fortune in the near future. Creative energy is at your service.
- If you want a significant relationship, there is a good chance of success.
- If you must go to court, don't worry. The judgement will be in your favor.
- Don't change your home or homeland. It will bring you no advantage.
- If you are sick, you will soon get well again.

Advice to the Wayfarer

Thank your creative spirit for the happiness it has bestowed on you. You can feel secure in all you do. If you are called on to act, draw on the gifts the spirit gave you. People will treasure you and gladly cluster around you. **Dharma**: give thanks for Heaven's grace by giving freely to others.

• 43 HEAVEN AND EARTH

Heaven and earth in complete harmony.
The Myriad Beings grow and thrive.
Peace and satisfaction prevail,
for blessings and wisdom are given to all.

) *Waning Moon: Emerging Yin*

This is the time to harvest. It will bring insight as well as profit.
Reap and gather your crops. Conserve your energy and nourish the
spirits. Honor the experienced.

Season: Autumn & the West *Element*: Metal

Symbols: Mists & Heaven

Life Cycle: the Elders

You have sown compassion and you reap the harvest of joy and love.
What a gift you have been given!

What Can and Cannot Happen

- Your family is harmonious and stable and you have yourself to
  thank for it.
- Your business ideas are both possible and profitable. Count on
  a considerable income in the future. Gather and concentrate
  creative energy.
- If you want a significant relationship, commit yourself now.
  This will be a happy union.
- If you want an heir, you will soon have one.
- If you are planning a trip, be careful. You may be caught in dif-
  ficulties.
- Go to court if you must, for the judgement will be in your
  favor.

- If you want to change your home, go ahead. You have everything to gain.
- Your health is unstable. See a doctor to clarify the problems.

Advice to the Wayfarer

Anything you wish to do stands under a lucky star. Grasp the opportunity with both hands, so your many ideas can be developed. You don't have to hurry, for success will come without you exhausting yourself. **Dharma**: the soul of sweet delight can never be defiled.

• 44 Diamond against Diamond

Diamond cuts diamond.
A Master
finds a daunting opponent.
How can you tell the winner from the loser?

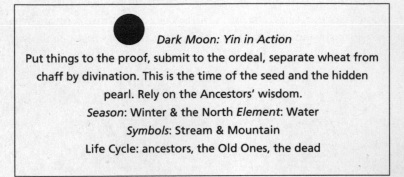

Dark Moon: Yin in Action
Put things to the proof, submit to the ordeal, separate wheat from chaff by divination. This is the time of the seed and the hidden pearl. Rely on the Ancestors' wisdom.
Season: Winter & the North *Element*: Water
Symbols: Stream & Mountain
Life Cycle: ancestors, the Old Ones, the dead

The test of skill and integrity. Put yourself to the proof and find the seed of things to come.

What Can and Cannot Happen

- Your household is secure and in perfect order. You have a happy home to call your own.
- Business affairs are running like a dream. If you keep on, you can count on a very significant profit. Find the hidden creative energy.
- If you try to force a significant relationship at any cost, your plans will go wrong. Put your desires off until later.
- Don't go to court. Settle your conflicts through arbitration and reconciliation.
- Take care of your health. An illness now could bring complications.

Advice to the Wayfarer

You are confronting a powerful opponent. You must act with foresight and strategy. Make no mistakes! In a desperate game of chess, the one who plays with both spirit and reflection will win. As long as you don't underestimate your opponent, there is no reason to fear. **Dharma**: prepare carefully to act spontaneously.

• 45 PATIENCE AND INTELLIGENCE

> Patience and intelligence
> will always triumph
> over violent force
> and brute strength.

(*Waxing Moon: Emerging Yang*

This is the source of energy and power, the origin of sexual drives.
Use it to unfold your plans. Rouse things, help them emerge and
flower. Free yourself and play.

Season: Spring & the East *Element*: Wood

Symbols: Thunder, Wind & Wood

Life Cycle: birth & childhood

---

*If you can free yourself from the desire for force and power, this can be a
very fertile time.*

What Can and Cannot Happen

- Your household is the image of a happy family and you feel protected by its harmony. There are no signs that this will change.
- Business looks very good. Expect a significant increase in profit in the near future. Creative energy is on the rise.
- If you wish, you can soon begin a significant relationship.
- If you must go to court, the judgement will be in your favor.
- If you are worried about your health, see a doctor now. If you are sick, don't worry. You will soon be well again.

Advice to the Wayfarer

You are kind and warmhearted and can count on people being willing to help you. Destiny will also be kind, so all your plans will turn out well. Have confidence, but don't be carried away by success. Stay just the way you are! **Dharma**: take refuge in the Buddha, the Teaching and the Community of Seekers.

● 46 FLOWERS FROM A WITHERED TREE

Even a withered tree will bloom again one day.
Count on the rhythms of nature.
Stay still for now
and let things be just as they are.

◯ *Full Moon: Yang in Action*
Everything grows, matures and ripens, vigorous and effective.
Unfold and complete your plans and watch them bear fruit. Care
for the children.
Season: Summer & the South *Element*: Fire
Symbols: Brightness & Warmth
Life Cycle: adults, parents

This is the time when the long forgotten hopes and dreams finally bear fruit. Simply let go and enjoy them.

What Can and Cannot Happen

- Everything in your house and family is going just as it should. There is no need to make changes except in small ways.
- You have the prospect of considerable business success in the long run. Hold back and wait for the right opportunity. Creative energy is at your service.
- If you want a significant relationship, your wish will soon come true. Talk to your friend as soon as you can.
- If you are expecting a child, it will be a daughter.
- If you must go to court, the judgement will be in your favor.
- Don't change your home. Dig your roots in deeper where you are now.
- If you are worried about your health, go to a doctor immediately.

Advice to the Wayfarer

You can do nothing at the moment, for the situation is very insecure. If you try to push forward, it will undoubtedly turn out badly. Carefully observe what is going on around you. Be patient, even when it is difficult. **Dharma**: invoke the Protector and wait for her aid.

• 47 THE EMPEROR'S EXAMINATION

It is never too late for honor and fame.
Return to yourself.
You will pass the Emperor's Examination.
It is written in your stars.

>)) *Waning Moon: Emerging Yin*
> This is the time to harvest. It will bring insight as well as profit.
> Reap and gather your crops. Conserve your energy and nourish the
> spirits. Honor the experienced.
> *Season*: Autumn & the West *Element*: Metal
> *Symbols*: Mists & Heaven
> Life Cycle: the Elders

---

*Wake up, Noble One! You are living beneath yourself. It is never too
late to return to the Way. Concentrate your insight.*

What Can and Cannot Happen

- Give more time to your family. Difficulties are brewing, but you can head them off.
- Business is difficult, but if you persevere firmly the outlook is good. Gather and concentrate creative energy.
- If you want a significant relationship, a lucky star will bless the union.
- If you want an heir, you will soon have one.
- Try to avoid going to court. If you must do so, however, the judgement will be in your favor.
- Think about changing your home. It may be a wise thing to do.
- If you are not well, go to a doctor now. It could take a long time to recover.

Advice to the Wayfarer

Why have you taken on a life and a destiny that are not yours at all? You are living far below yourself. You are gifted and energetic, though you lack a certain ambition and, above all, endurance. Make new plans, your old ones are useless. You will soon see a smooth transition from your present situation to something completely new. **Dharma**: think of your karma. The way of the world is not *always* bad.

• 48 MILES OF CLOUDS

One autumn day, a partridge changed itself into a dragon.
What other kind of bird enjoys such freedom?
It flew higher and higher through miles of white clouds,
until it was floating in heaven.

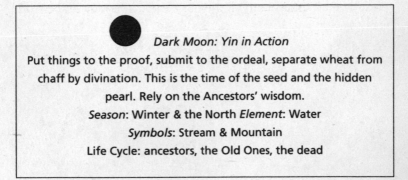

Dark Moon: Yin in Action

Put things to the proof, submit to the ordeal, separate wheat from chaff by divination. This is the time of the seed and the hidden pearl. Rely on the Ancestors' wisdom.
Season: Winter & the North *Element*: Water
Symbols: Stream & Mountain
Life Cycle: ancestors, the Old Ones, the dead

You find that you can really ride the dragon energy. Step on and begin the long heavenly journey. Don't look back and don't look down.

What Can and Cannot Happen

- Your household is peaceful and calm and this will not soon change. Everyone feels protected in the bosom of the family.
- You are waiting for the sale of a concern to bring you a large profit. Hold back for now and don't be upset. Success won't come until autumn. Find the hidden creative energy.
- You cannot begin a significant relationship in the near future.
- If you are expecting a child, all will go well with no complications.
- If you must go to court, don't worry. The judgement will go in your favor.
- If you are ill, don't worry. You will soon be well again.

Advice to the Wayfarer

A great change stands before you, but you must fly through miles and miles of white clouds before you get there. Don't expect immediate results, but don't worry. What you really need is patience. **Dharma**: the song of the Jewel in the Lotus will bring the sky goddesses to your aid!

• 49 ICE THAT TURNS TO WATER

> The chilly waters turn to ice
> when the year gets colder.
> One day the ice
> will turn to flowing water again.

Waxing Moon: Emerging Yang

This is the source of energy and power, the origin of sexual drives.
Use it to unfold your plans. Rouse things, help them emerge and
flower. Free yourself and play.
Season: Spring & the East *Element*: Wood
Symbols: Thunder, Wind & Wood
Life Cycle: birth & childhood

---

*Feelings long frozen melt in the soft winds of spring. Open your heart
and you will burst into bloom.*

What Can and Cannot Happen

- Investigate what is happening in your family. Why is everyone so disturbed? There are hidden tensions and conflicts at work.
- Obstacles plague your business transactions. There are no easy profits at the moment. Creative energy is on the rise.
- If you are thinking of beginning a significant relationship, you must think again. Is this partner right for you? It is not likely that you would be happy.
- If you are expecting a child, have a doctor watch over the whole pregnancy.
- Don't take your adversary to court. It will cost much more than you think and will rule out the possibility of an out-of-court compromise.

- Don't plan to change your home now. A new place will make things worse.
- If you fall ill, your condition could last for quite a while.

Advice to the Wayfarer

At the moment, things don't look too rosy. You feel stuck, without energy, like you were fettered and chained. Be cautious and don't start anything you haven't thoroughly considered. If you follow this simple advice and don't act on impulse, you will soon see things getting better. **Dharma**: stone walls do not a prison make. Cleanse your heart before you act.

• 50 THE OPEN SEA

> With swelling sails the boat glides
> over the limitless open sea.
> When the wind is steady in the right quarter,
> she will return home laden with jade and priceless jewels.

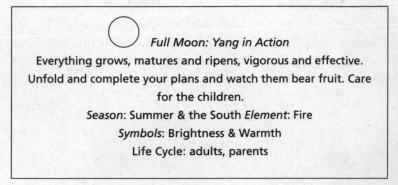

Full Moon: Yang in Action
Everything grows, matures and ripens, vigorous and effective.
Unfold and complete your plans and watch them bear fruit. Care
for the children.
Season: Summer & the South *Element*: Fire
Symbols: Brightness & Warmth
Life Cycle: adults, parents

*An endless voyage on the summer seas, while the fruits of
happiness ripen.*

What Can and Cannot Happen

- Congratulations! Your household is in perfect order, full of joy and sunshine.
- See if you can put off selling your business as you planned. Creative energy is at your service. You will find your luck in the West.
- Don't begin a significant relationship yet, for your partner isn't clear about their desires and needs.
- If you are expecting a child, all will go well.
- Don't go to court, for the judgement will go against you.
- Don't change your home. It will only turn out for the worst.
- If you are sick, don't worry. You will soon be well again.

Advice to the Wayfarer

Your life is comfortable and agreeable. The future holds nothing too strenuous, for luck is with you on your journey through life. Beware of arousing people's envy. Always be well informed about things, especially when you have the sudden urge to share your good fortune with others. **Dharma**: the treasure hard to attain lies always within reach.

• 51 THE SUMMER SUN

The scorching heat of long summer days –
a torture we all must endure.
How lovely, when a fresh breeze blows.
The benevolence of Heaven caresses the human soul.

Waning Moon: Emerging Yin

This is the time to harvest. It will bring insight as well as profit.
Reap and gather your crops. Conserve your energy and nourish the
spirits. Honor the experienced.

Season: Autumn & the West *Element*: Metal

Symbols: Mists & Heaven

Life Cycle: the Elders

Help is on its way. Concentrate your insight and free yourself from the illusion of obstacles.

What Can and Cannot Happen

- You can be truly satisfied with your household and family. There is no sign that this will change.
- Your business is in order. There is no sign of change, positive or negative. Autumn may bring good fortune. Gather and concentrate creative energy.
- If you want to begin a significant relationship, your plans will bear fruit.
- If you are expecting a child, it will be a son.
- Your guests will appear soon. They are already on the way.
- If you must go to court, the judgement will be in your favor.
- A change of home will bring you no advantage.

- If you feel unwell, see a doctor. Without help, you will not recover quickly.

Advice to the Wayfarer

You are currently in difficulties that, fortunately, aren't too serious. Do not lose your patience under any circumstances. It won't be long before your troubles solve themselves. A talk with a friend would really help, for you would get good advice. **Dharma**: ask the Protector again how you can change your situation.

● 52 MOON IN THE WATER

> The moon shines
> bright and clear in the water.
> You think you can reach out and touch it,
> but it is only an illusion.

Dark Moon: Yin in Action

Put things to the proof, submit to the ordeal, separate wheat from chaff by divination. This is the time of the seed and the hidden pearl. Rely on the Ancestors' wisdom.

Season: Winter & the North *Element*: Water

Symbols: Stream & Mountain

Life Cycle: ancestors, the Old Ones, the dead

You are deluding yourself in your current goals. Try to see behind them to find the hidden treasure.

What Can and Cannot Happen

- Your family is disordered, confused and strained. There is no clear goal for anyone to pursue.
- There are so many business obstacles now that you cannot count on improving your finances. Find the hidden creative energy.
- Obstacles will prevent you from beginning a significant relationship. Hold back for now!
- If you expect a child, beware complications. Take adequate precautions.
- If you are involved in litigation, avoid going to court. Try to settle through a compromise.
- If you want to move or leave the country, hold back for now. It could turn out to your disadvantage.

- If you are sick, don't worry. You will soon be on your feet again.

Advice to the Wayfarer

Don't spread gossip or scandal and you won't irritate other people or put yourself in a compromising position. Concentrate your attention on your family situation. When that is in order, you can breathe again. **Dharma**: you must learn the nature of illusion, or this will happen again and again!

● 53 THE TIGER'S ROAR

The tiger's roar resounds.
He is satisfied with himself.
The dragon, however,
hisses with irritation to hear him.

Waxing Moon: Emerging Yang

This is the source of energy and power, the origin of sexual drives.
Use it to unfold your plans. Rouse things, help them emerge and
flower. Free yourself and play.

Season: Spring & the East *Element*: Wood

Symbols: Thunder, Wind & Wood

Life Cycle: birth & childhood

---

*Stop seeing things in terms of yes and no, black and white, and the
world will suddenly blossom.*

What Can and Cannot Happen

- Your household is not happy, but it is not so dramatic. Give more attention to family matters.
- Business is not running smoothly, so don't count on any special success. Creative energy is on the rise.
- If you are beginning a significant relationship, congratulations! It will be very happy and harmonious.
- If you expect guests, they will soon arrive.
- There is no need to go to court. Settle this matter in a friendly fashion.
- If you are sick, don't be frightened. You will soon be well.

Advice to the Wayfarer

It looks like everything has come to a halt, but don't lose courage. Destiny has success in mind for you. Go your way calmly and don't let go of your ideas and ideals. **Dharma**: light is the left hand of darkness, darkness the left hand of light.

• 54 SHIFTING REFLECTIONS

> Trees and bushes
> reflected in the running water.
> Their image shifts and changes
> creating confusion in the mind.

◯ *Full Moon: Yang in Action*

**Everything grows, matures and ripens, vigorous and effective.
Unfold and complete your plans and watch them bear fruit. Care
for the children.**

Season: Summer & the South *Element*: Fire

Symbols: Brightness & Warmth

Life Cycle: adults, parents

---

*You are confused by a mad whirl of activity. Stop. Take a breath. Find
the center and let things ripen on their own.*

What Can and Cannot Happen

- Your household and family are at odds. Take measures to overcome the confusion.
- You will encounter many business obstacles before you can count on a profit. Creative energy is at your service.
- Your plans for a significant relationship will probably not succeed.
- If you are expecting a child, be careful. You should be under a doctor's care.
- Don't go to court on any account! Your case would simply be thrown out.
- If you are under a doctor's care, ask yourself if he or she is really the right one for you.

Advice to the Wayfarer

You are in a difficult situation. You have to take things as they are for now, you simply can't change them. Above all, be clear about your situation as a basis for the next step. Don't be afraid to make a radical change when you come to a resolution. **Dharma**: invoke the Noble Protectors to guard your thoughts and speech.

• 55 THE ETERNAL SPRING

A long row of bamboo stalks
joined together
reaches to a bubbling spring.
Generation after generation can draw on the water.

)) *Waning Moon: Emerging Yin*

This is the time to harvest. It will bring insight as well as profit.
Reap and gather your crops. Conserve your energy and nourish the
spirits. Honor the experienced.

Season: Autumn & the West *Element*: Metal

Symbols: Mists & Heaven

Life Cycle: the Elders

---

*Concentrate your energy and insight. Your efforts now can benefit many
people and extend to future generations.*

What Can and Cannot Happen

- There is a misunderstanding in your family. Clear it up as soon as you can.
- You will enjoy great business success. Profits will soar. Gather and concentrate creative energy.
- If you haven't been able to persuade your friend into a significant relationship, try again! A union with this person is under a lucky star.
- If you are expecting a child, all will go smoothly.
- If you must go to court, you can count on the help of an influential person. The judgement will be in your favor.

- Go through with your change of home. Everything will benefit.
- If you are sick, you will soon recover.

Advice to the Wayfarer

Everything is in flux. Be happy that destiny has chosen you for success. Work untroubled at your goals and trust yourself and your destiny. Your self-confidence will be very useful. **Dharma**: dedicate your work to the happiness of all sentient beings.

• 56 MOONBEAMS AND EVENING FLOWERS

The beauty of moonbeams, the cool evening breeze,
the soft murmur of a stream refresh us.
But don't let yourself be distracted
by the charming flowers and trees.

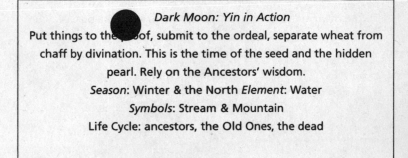

Dark Moon: Yin in Action
Put things to the proof, submit to the ordeal, separate wheat from
chaff by divination. This is the time of the seed and the hidden
pearl. Rely on the Ancestors' wisdom.
Season: Winter & the North *Element*: Water
Symbols: Stream & Mountain
Life Cycle: ancestors, the Old Ones, the dead

*Don't be distracted by the passing play of sweet illusion. Concentrate on
the treasure hidden within.*

What Can and Cannot Happen

- Be grateful that your family is happy and peaceful. It isn't always that way.
- This is a good time for business. You stand a chance to make a very sizable profit. Find the hidden creative energy.
- If you want a significant relationship, your plans will be accomplished.
- If you wish for an heir, you will soon have one.
- If you are involved in litigation, you can go to court with confidence. The judgement will go in your favor.
- If you want to move or leave the country, all signs are positive.
- If you are sick, don't worry. You will soon be sound as a nut.

Advice to the Wayfarer

You have many plans but don't know which to choose. First decide which are wishes and fantasies and which are real ideas. Once you have chosen, don't be distracted or stray down a path you haven't chosen. **Dharma**: distance yourself from the compulsive need for beauty.

• 57 Gifts of Fate

Destiny is giving you abundance.
Go on your way
with happiness and success as companions.
Leave the cares and sorrows of the past behind.

Waxing Moon: Emerging Yang

This is the source of energy and power, the origin of sexual drives.
Use it to unfold your plans. Rouse things, help them emerge and
flower. Free yourself and play.

Season: Spring & the East *Element*: Wood

Symbols: Thunder, Wind & Wood

Life Cycle: birth & childhood

Fate has given you this wonderful time, a new birth, to enjoy and share.
Leave the ghosts of the past and step into the future.

What Can and Cannot Happen

- The atmosphere of your household is troubled. Be careful about your relations and avoid all kinds of scandal and gossip.
- Business prospects are extraordinarily good. Count on success and an extraordinary rise in profits in the near future. Creative energy is on the rise.
- A significant relationship could develop smoothly and quickly.
- If you are expecting a child, it will be a daughter.
- Don't go to court! Settle your affairs in a friendly fashion.
- Don't change your home now. It will bring you no advantage and will cost much more than you expect.

Advice to the Wayfarer

Be methodical in everything. Don't get caught up in scandal and gossip, for it will only complicate your life. Forget the past and enjoy the present. You will soon be happy and satisfied again. **Dharma**: honor the Goddess of Compassion as you walk on your path.

• 58 FOREIGN LANDS

Don't seek your luck in foreign lands.
There is no chance to better your lot there.
Be patient and stay right where you are.
All will come good in the end.

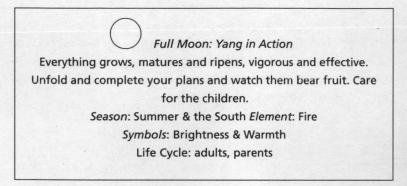

Full Moon: Yang in Action
**Everything grows, matures and ripens, vigorous and effective.
Unfold and complete your plans and watch them bear fruit. Care
for the children.
Season: Summer & the South *Element*: Fire
Symbols: Brightness & Warmth
Life Cycle: adults, parents**

Things are ripening right here at home. Why do you need to travel?

What Can and Cannot Happen

- Nothing special is happening in your family and no changes are in sight.
- If you take the long view, your business will be very successful. You can improve your profits significantly. Creative energy is at your service.
- If you want a significant relationship, don't count on quick results.
- If you are expecting a child, take precautions against complications.
- If you are expecting guests, they will arrive later than you think.
- Stay where you are now. A change of home is not advisable.
- If you are ill, go to a doctor.

Advice to the Wayfarer

You are impatient and restless. Why? Why use force when there are real opportunities open to you? When you try too hard you could easily be harmed. What you need is patience and still more patience! **Dharma**: if you can see the myriad worlds in a grain of sand, why do you need to stir?

• 59 THE THORNY JUNGLE

Climbing a tower
when you want to hide
makes about as much sense as holding your breath
because you are trapped in a thorny jungle.

)) *Waning Moon: Emerging Yin*

This is the time to harvest. It will bring insight as well as profit.
Reap and gather your crops. Conserve your energy and nourish the
spirits. Honor the experienced.

Season: Autumn & the West *Element*: Metal

Symbols: Mists & Heaven

Life Cycle: the Elders

You are trapped in fear and hysteria. Wake up! Pull yourself together!
Concentrate your insight and reap the rewards.

What Can and Cannot Happen

- Your household is beset by difficulties that are not your fault. In any case, try to resolve them as soon as possible.
- Business affairs are in fairly good shape. Count on a significant improvement soon. Gather and concentrate creative energy.
- Chances of a significant relationship in the immediate future are very small.
- This is not a good time to have children.
- Don't go to court. The judgement will go against you.
- Changing your home could be greatly to your advantage.
- Be careful of your health and you will not become ill.

Advice to the Wayfarer

Take no risks now. Be patient, all will turn out to your advantage in the end. Be calm when people attack you and don't let anyone persuade you to do something against your will. **Dharma**: why look for fish in a vegetable market?

• 60 Throwing Oil on the Flames

If you throw oil on a fire
to put it out
or if you carry firewood into a burning house,
the flames will only blaze higher.

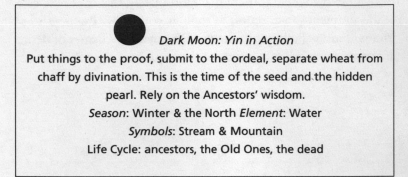

Dark Moon: Yin in Action

Put things to the proof, submit to the ordeal, separate wheat from chaff by divination. This is the time of the seed and the hidden pearl. Rely on the Ancestors' wisdom.
Season: **Winter & the North** *Element*: **Water**
Symbols: Stream & Mountain
Life Cycle: ancestors, the Old Ones, the dead

If you foolishly add fuel to the flames of your passions, the treasure hidden within will be burned away.

What Can and Cannot Happen

- Your household is in danger. Tensions are building to a breaking point. Take precautions as soon as possible before open dissension explodes.
- Don't expect any improvement in financial affairs. Business deals have little chance of success at the moment. Find the hidden creative energy.
- You stand little chance of a significant relationship at a time like this.
- If you are expecting a child, be careful and seek advice.
- If you go to court, the judgement will certainly go against you.
- If you are planning to move, you may find the source of all your problems.

• If you are sick, go to a good doctor now. Recovery may take quite a while.

Advice to the Wayfarer

Your situation is in flux. Defend yourself from attack on all sides. Cultivate equilibrium and calm in both private and public life so that you know where you stand. Unfortunately, that is not the case at the moment. Take action as soon as you know the next step. You will soon climb out of the pit. **Dharma**: the flames of desire are never-ending. Only insight and compassion can still them.

• 61 CELEBRATE LIFE!

> Why do we hide? Why don't we celebrate
> when the time comes to enjoy life?
> Life is full of both good and bad
> and no one knows his destiny.

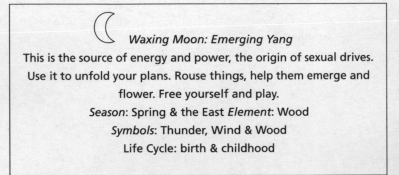

Waxing Moon: Emerging Yang

This is the source of energy and power, the origin of sexual drives.
Use it to unfold your plans. Rouse things, help them emerge and
flower. Free yourself and play.

Season: Spring & the East *Element*: Wood

Symbols: Thunder, Wind & Wood

Life Cycle: birth & childhood

*Now is the time to celebrate life, love, joy and desire. Open your heart
to the new rebirth of wonder!*

What Can and Cannot Happen

- Enjoy your happy home. You have your own efforts to thank for it!
- Your business is running smoothly and your income will grow. Creative energy is on the rise.
- If you wish for a significant relationship, the union will be under a lucky star.
- If you are expecting a child, it will be a daughter.
- If you must go to court, the judgement will go in your favor.
- If you don't feel comfortable where you are, don't hesitate to move. It will turn out to your advantage.
- If you are sick, don't worry. You will soon be in good form again.

Advice to the Wayfarer

Everything is very prosperous. Be happy that you are not plagued by a host of troubles, but don't simply sit back and enjoy it. Something has fallen into your hand. Take hold of the opportunity and use it. **Dharma**: effort bears fruit when joy and sorrow are one path.

• 62 THE NOBLE FRIEND

A true friend and protector stands by you.
Through his help
you will become a person of consequence,
both respected and rich.

Full Moon: Yang in Action
**Everything grows, matures and ripens, vigorous and effective.
Unfold and complete your plans and watch them bear fruit. Care
for the children.**
***Season**: Summer & the South **Element**: Fire*
***Symbols**: Brightness & Warmth*
Life Cycle: adults, parents

*Things grow to maturity through the help of the noble truths. Let your
higher self bear fruit.*

What Can and Cannot Happen

- Your household is happy and you can depend on it staying that way.
- You will be successful in business without really trying. Creative energy is at your service.
- If you want a significant relationship, your plans will quickly bear fruit.
- If you are expecting a child, be careful. There may be complications, so let a good doctor help you.
- Be careful on trips. You could get caught up in difficulties.
- If you are involved in litigation, don't go to court. Your case is not sound and the judgement will go against you.

- Don't change your home. You are secure and happy where you are now.
- If you have troubles with your health, don't worry. You will soon recover.

Advice to the Wayfarer

You are entering a very fortunate time, when all your hidden apprehensions and fears will prove to be illusions. Forget the past and concentrate on the future. Have no cares. When you set out on your new path, everything will turn out to your satisfaction. **Dharma**: take refuge in the Great Protector and past lives dissolve like the mists.

• 63 THE LOST COMPASS

Unfortunately, you lost your compass on your last voyage.
You must do without it now.
Even if you found it, it would have little meaning.
It is too late. You cannot reach your goal.

) *Waning Moon: Emerging Yin*

This is the time to harvest. It will bring insight as well as profit.
Reap and gather your crops. Conserve your energy and nourish the
spirits. Honor the experienced.
Season: Autumn & the West *Element*: Metal
Symbols: Mists & Heaven
Life Cycle: the Elders

---

*You are scattered and directionless. Concentrate your insight. Pull
yourself together and reap the rewards.*

What Can and Cannot Happen

- A sudden difficulty will appear in your household. Prepare
  yourself so you won't be surprised.
- Your business is successful and prosperity will increase. Gather
  and concentrate creative energy.
- Your desire for a significant relationship won't work out right
  now.
- This is not the time for children, but don't be discouraged.
- Don't go to court, for the judgement will go against you. Seek
  a compromise.
- If you feel uncomfortable in your home, change it quickly.
- If you are sick, see a doctor.

Advice to the Wayfarer

Things seem hopeless and you think all your efforts have been in vain. Don't despair. Exert yourself! You will soon make a fortunate move that will put you on the road to success. Always keep your goal in mind. **Dharma**: what does the ignorant one do? Chop wood and carry water. What does the enlightened one do? Chop wood and carry water.

• 64 CAUGHT IN THE NET

In a muddy pool a fish caught in a net,
closed in on all sides.
He can find no way out even when he struggles.
All his efforts are in vain.

Dark Moon: Yin in Action

Put things to the proof, submit to the ordeal, separate wheat from
chaff by divination. This is the time of the seed and the hidden
pearl. Rely on the Ancestors' wisdom.
Season: Winter & the North *Element*: Water
Symbols: Stream & Mountain
Life Cycle: ancestors, the Old Ones, the dead

You are trapped. The only way out is the way in to the hidden treasure.

What Can and Cannot Happen

- Your household is full of tension that could break out any minute. Beware!
- Your financial condition is not too good, though business transactions may soon give you hope. Find the hidden creative energy.
- Don't go to court under any condition. There is no chance that you could win.
- If you want to change your home, go through with your plans. They will work very much to your advantage.
- If you are ill, be careful! Seek a doctor now or the cure will take a long time.

Advice to the Wayfarer

Be careful in all you do, or you will be caught in an impossible situation. Even when things seem secure, something could happen that you are unable to cope with. Prepare yourself against the unforeseen. **Dharma**: change your heart! Call on the Protector to help you.

• 65 AN IDIOT'S CURE

Only an idiot
would cut off his own flesh
to cure a wound.
It will only cause him more pain.

(*Waxing Moon: Emerging Yang*
This is the source of energy and power, the origin of sexual drives.
Use it to unfold your plans. Rouse things, help them emerge and
flower. Free yourself and play.
Season: Spring & the East *Element*: Wood
Symbols: Thunder, Wind & Wood
Life Cycle: birth & childhood

If you can free yourself from obstinacy and ignorance, this can be a very fertile time.

What Can and Cannot Happen

- Your household is quite turbulent. Put things in order and restore peace.
- Be careful in business transactions. Your success could be ruined through envy. Creative energy is on the rise.
- Your desire for a significant relationship will lead to unhappiness. This is not the partner for you.
- If you are expecting a child, seek a doctor's care to avoid complications.
- Don't go to court, for the judgement will go against you.
- Don't change your home. You are most secure where you are now.
- If you are sick, see a specialist. Only he can cure you.

Advice to the Wayfarer

Beware of criticism, for it can harm you now. Don't make any significant changes. Your situation is neither dangerous nor safe, so don't be impatient. Rein yourself in for a while. **Dharma**: one yin, one yang is the way. Act without acting and you arrive at the goal.

• 66 THE SINKING SHIP

Like a battered ship
that sinks in the stormy sea,
the sun fades into the evening sky.
All that is left are withered, frozen leaves.

○ *Full Moon: Yang in Action*
Everything grows, matures and ripens, vigorous and effective.
Unfold and complete your plans and watch them bear fruit. Care
for the children.
Season: Summer & the South *Element*: Fire
Symbols: Brightness & Warmth
Life Cycle: adults, parents

Caught in a mindless swirl of activity, you see all your hopes founder.
Stop. Calm yourself and wait for the change of season.

What Can and Cannot Happen

- Your household is full of tension and mistrust. Stake everything on re-establishing peace.
- The business outlook is not so rosy. You may be in financial danger. Creative energy is at your service.
- Your significant relationship is in trouble. Be patient and circumspect and it won't founder.
- Don't go to court. You will surely lose your case.
- If you want to change your home, put your plans on hold for now. A change will only bring new difficulties.
- If you are sick, be sure to find a good doctor.

Advice to the Wayfarer

Your situation is so precarious that you must constantly be on guard. Take precautions. Change nothing. Make no plans. The time is not right to take action, so wait! If you hold back, success won't take long to appear. **Dharma**: strengthen your heart through compassion and insight.

• 67 PEACE AND ORDER

Don't play favorites to your own advantage.
Let the righteous person make the choice.
Things endure through honesty.
Do what is right so peace may prevail.

) *Waning Moon: Emerging Yin*

This is the time to harvest. It will bring insight as well as profit.
Reap and gather your crops. Conserve your energy and nourish the
spirits. Honor the experienced.

Season: Autumn & the West *Element*: Metal

Symbols: Mists & Heaven

Life Cycle: the Elders

Disentangle yourself from greed and let the natural balance be re-established. Concentrate your insight and reap the rewards.

What Can and Cannot Happen

- Your household is running smoothly and harmoniously. You can feel secure in your home.
- You have few business opportunities now. Be careful in all your dealings. Gather and concentrate creative energy.
- If you wish for a significant relationship, your plans will soon be successful.
- If you wish for an heir, you will have one.
- Don't go to court. Settle things in a friendly fashion.
- If you plan a change of home, it would be better to give it up. It would bring you no advantage.
- If you are sick, don't worry. You will soon be well.

Advice to the Wayfarer

Be calm and cautious in all you do. Don't be critical and demanding. Pursue your goal, but not at the expense of family and friends. That would cost you heavily in the long run. Stay unbiased and honest. Your world will be better for it. **Dharma**: distance yourself from greed and the lust for power.

• 68 SPRING DAYS

When spring comes
and the days grow longer,
the flowers bloom more and more luxuriously.
All is set free at last.

Dark Moon: Yin in Action

Put things to the proof, submit to the ordeal, separate wheat from chaff by divination. This is the time of the seed and the hidden pearl. Rely on the Ancestors' wisdom.

Season: Winter & the North *Element*: Water

Symbols: Stream & Mountain

Life Cycle: ancestors, the Old Ones, the dead

You have found the hidden treasure. Wait for the new season to unfold a new way of living.

What Can and Cannot Happen

- Your family enjoys an extraordinary understanding with each other, an understanding that includes your circle of friends.
- Business success is guaranteed. The new year will bring you extraordinary profits. Find the hidden creative energy.
- If you wish for a significant relationship, don't delay. It will be very happy.
- If you are expecting a child, be very careful. Seek a doctor's advice.
- If you expect guests, they will arrive at the appointed time.
- Don't go to court, for the judgement will go against you.
- You are probably in the process of changing your home. This move will prove very advantageous.
- Your sickness will soon be cured through a special medicine.

Advice to the Wayfarer

You are very lucky. Everything you do will be successful and all your hopes will be fulfilled. Don't lose any time. Set to work now! **Dharma**: skillful means bring a far-reaching change.

• 69 THE PLUM TREE IN WINTER

A plum tree grows alone on the top of a hill.
Its leaves fall and its branches are heavy with frost.
When spring returns to warm the earth
it will regain its beauty and its kingdom.

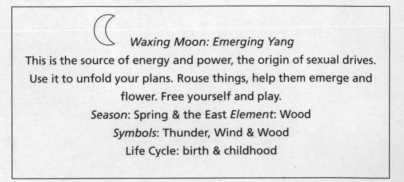

Waxing Moon: Emerging Yang
This is the source of energy and power, the origin of sexual drives.
Use it to unfold your plans. Rouse things, help them emerge and
flower. Free yourself and play.
Season: Spring & the East *Element*: Wood
Symbols: Thunder, Wind & Wood
Life Cycle: birth & childhood

*After a long, courageous and lonely struggle, the light will return to bless
and care for you. A new world of beauty will open and blossom.*

What Can and Cannot Happen

- Your present household arrangements will not last. Look for
  the first signs of the storm so you can take the right steps.
- Business prospects are not too good. Be careful in all your
  transactions so that you don't fall into a trap. Creative energy is
  on the rise.
- Your plans for a significant relationship won't go quickly, but
  don't be discouraged.
- If you wish for a child, it will arrive in spring rather than fall.
- If you are sick, go to a doctor immediately so the cure won't be
  delayed.

Advice to the Wayfarer

Your plans won't work out now, but don't be discouraged or depressed. Your lucky time will come. Be patient. If you get nervous, you will make a wrong decision that will come back to haunt you. **Dharma**: you have known a million million springs and a million million winters.

• 70 THE EAGER BEES

Each morning the bees fly here and there,
diligently sucking nectar from the glorious flowers.
When the flowers fade, they no longer have a purpose.
Endless rain washes the spring away.

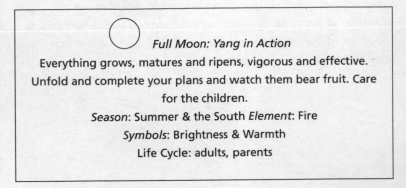

Full Moon: Yang in Action
Everything grows, matures and ripens, vigorous and effective.
Unfold and complete your plans and watch them bear fruit. Care
for the children.
Season: Summer & the South *Element*: Fire
Symbols: Brightness & Warmth
Life Cycle: adults, parents

*You are caught in an obsessive swirl of activity that will exhaust you if
you cannot calm yourself and expand your awareness.*

What Can and Cannot Happen

- Your household is full of gossip and scandal. Put a stop to it as soon as possible. Use all your energy. Above all, guard your family from evil outside influences.
- No luck in business for now. Guard yourself against losses. Creative energy is at your service.
- Your business partners are moody, oversensitive and untrustworthy. Don't rely on them.
- Don't begin a significant relationship, for it won't last.
- This is not the time to have children. Be patient.
- Don't become involved in legal matters. They will not turn out well.

- If you are sick, count on an operation. Drugs won't cure your problem.

Advice to the Wayfarer

You have very little given to you. You must work hard to earn a living. As long as your situation is uncertain, don't try to force the fulfillment of your wishes. Pull back a bit and wait for the right moment, when a real opportunity is offered to you. **Dharma**: the enlightened one works when there is work and stops when there is no work.

• 71 TWO ARROWS ON ONE BOW

A woman should not give herself to two suitors.
One will always founder.
A dragon and a unicorn fight when they come together.
How can two arrows be shot from one bow?

)) *Waning Moon: Emerging Yin*
This is the time to harvest. It will bring insight as well as profit.
Reap and gather your crops. Conserve your energy and nourish the
spirits. Honor the experienced.
Season: Autumn & the West *Element*: Metal
Symbols: Mists & Heaven
Life Cycle: the Elders

You must choose between two things. You cannot have both.
Concentrate your insight and reap the rewards.

What Can and Cannot Happen

- Your family is disturbed and scandal has broken out. Try to make the way smooth again.
- Business affairs are not good, but you will be able to live with it. Don't count on making a fortune just yet. Gather and concentrate creative energy.
- Your significant relationship is falling apart, but reconciliation is still possible. Try for it with all your might.
- If you are expecting a child and this is a first birth, be careful and seek advice.
- Don't go to court, for the judgement will surely go against you.
- Be careful of your health. There is the danger of a lingering illness.

Advice to the Wayfarer

Destiny has mapped out your next steps, but that doesn't mean you have nothing to do! Think your relationships over calmly and carefully so you can eliminate the unnecessary. In business, don't be idle. Be active and consistent in pursuing all your goals. Suddenly you will find you have achieved everything you were striving for. **Dharma**: if you are always of two minds, you will live on a battlefield. Still the Monkey thoughts!

• 72 THE HONEY AND THE STING

Whoever hunts bees
for their honey
will feel their sting
from time to time.

Dark Moon: Yin in Action

Put things to the proof, submit to the ordeal, separate wheat from chaff by divination. This is the time of the seed and the hidden pearl. Rely on the Ancestors' wisdom.

Season: Winter & the North *Element*: Water

Symbols: Stream & Mountain

Life Cycle: ancestors, the Old Ones, the dead

Joy and sorrow go hand in hand. Realize this and you have found the hidden treasure.

What Can and Cannot Happen

- Struggle with the difficulties in your household so that the conflicts that plague your family can be resolved as soon as possible.
- Your finances will only get better through hard work. Find the hidden creative energy.
- Don't push your desire for a significant relationship. Use tact and reserve to carry out your plans.
- If you wish for children, you will soon see the first signs.
- Don't change your home. Living in a new place would be very difficult.
- Don't worry about your health. If you are sick, seek advice, but don't worry unnecessarily.

Advice to the Wayfarer

Your situation will only get better if you work at it. Although there are other ways to success, they would leave your thorny problems unsolved. Think over each step in your undertaking before you put it into action. Don't get stuck, for you need to keep your choices open. **Dharma**: pleasure and pain are close companions. You can't have one without the other.

• 73 SUDDEN THUNDER

Sudden spring thunder wakes the insects and the worms.
They sing together gaily and dance in a circle,
free from winter hibernation
deep in the earth.

Waxing Moon: Emerging Yang

This is the source of energy and power, the origin of sexual drives.
Use it to unfold your plans. Rouse things, help them emerge and
flower. Free yourself and play.

Season: Spring & the East *Element*: Wood

Symbols: Thunder, Wind & Wood

Life Cycle: birth & childhood

This is a time of deep awakening of joy and the release of long-buried feelings.

What Can and Cannot Happen

- Your household and family are doing very well. You feel a deep peace in the bosom of their love.
- Business prospects are extremely good. Next spring your profits will be extraordinary. Creative energy is on the rise.
- Your significant relationship is happy and this happiness will not change.
- Changing your home will bring many advantages.
- If you feel unwell, go to a doctor now so the sickness doesn't linger.

Advice to the Wayfarer

Everything you do stands under a lucky star and circumstances favor your plans. There could be a sudden change that fulfills your wishes in one stroke, perhaps more than you ever dreamed possible. **Dharma**: the Enlightened One remembers sorrow in joy and joy in sorrow. The way of life is always mixed.

• 74 LOSING YOUR WAY

> While looking for shelter,
> a snow goose inadvertently lost her way,
> stumbled into a cage
> and was trapped.

Full Moon: Yang in Action

Everything grows, matures and ripens, vigorous and effective.
Unfold and complete your plans and watch them bear fruit. Care
for the children.

Season: Summer & the South *Element*: Fire

Symbols: Brightness & Warmth

Life Cycle: adults, parents

You are trapped in a vicious circle of old ideas and negative feelings.
Take clear vigorous action and you can break through.

What Can and Cannot Happen

- Your household and family are in disorder and you have played a considerable part in creating the tension. Correct this situation as soon as possible so order can be restored.
- Competitors with bad intentions are trying to destroy your business. Be on your guard against financial loss. Creative energy is at your service.
- Your significant relationship stands on the razor's edge. Take care that no break occurs that could cause everyone suffering.
- Resolve conflicts out of court at all costs, for a judgement would certainly go against you.
- If you are sick, seek a specialist who will cure you swiftly and surely.

Advice to the Wayfarer

Go forward on all fronts. Don't pull back! Be energetic in pursuing your goals. Keep your judgement cool or you will run into trouble. This is a difficult time, but don't let yourself be influenced by it. Gather all your energy and courage and go on your way with a smile. **Dharma**: the greatest warriors are one with their weapons. They fight without killing and die without death.

• 75 Climb Mountain with Tiger

When you climb a mountain
with a tiger,
your heart pounds every moment
with the fear.

))) *Waning Moon: Emerging Yin*

This is the time to harvest. It will bring insight as well as profit.
Reap and gather your crops. Conserve your energy and nourish the
spirits. Honor the experienced.

Season: Autumn & the West *Element*: Metal

Symbols: Mists & Heaven

Life Cycle: the Elders

---

*This is a risky endeavor with a chance of great rewards. Concentrate
your insight. Always keep the tiger in your mind.*

What Can and Cannot Happen

- There is open difference of opinion in your household, but it is
  not impossible to overcome.
- Business prospects are not good. Take no risks now. Gather and
  concentrate creative energy.
- Your significant relationship is troubled. You must talk with
  your partner.
- If you are expecting a child, take precautions. Have a doctor
  present at the birth.
- In case of conflicts, come to terms at all costs. A judgement in
  court will certainly go against you.
- Have no worries over your health. If you fall ill, it will be a
  minor complaint.

Advice to the Wayfarer

The next period in your life will not be smooth. Protect yourself by taking certain precautions. Try to anticipate what will happen in everything you undertake. That way misfortune will not befall you. Don't insist on your so-called rights! **Dharma**: look in the mirror of the mind and you will see the tiger's face.

• 76 THE RIGHT OPPORTUNITY

One day opportunity will offer itself.
You will spring through the Dragon Door in one bound.
Wait for that opportunity
and you will fight your way free.

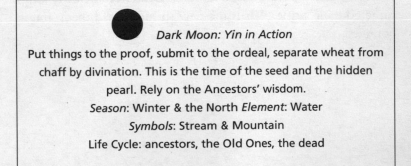

Dark Moon: Yin in Action

Put things to the proof, submit to the ordeal, separate wheat from
chaff by divination. This is the time of the seed and the hidden
pearl. Rely on the Ancestors' wisdom.
Season: Winter & the North *Element*: Water
Symbols: Stream & Mountain
Life Cycle: ancestors, the Old Ones, the dead

*Find the hidden treasure. This is the time to put everything to the test,
to sort out the real from the useless.*

What Can and Cannot Happen

- You couldn't wish for better in your household. Everyone is happy and in good health.
- You must be patient until success in business comes. You can count on very significant profits. Find the hidden creative energy.
- If you wish to begin a significant relationship, your wishes will come true if you are not impatient. Delay your desire for now.
- If you want an heir, you will soon have one.
- Don't go to court. The trial would last a long time without a judgement and would cost you much more than you expected.
- Change your home if you want to, but it will bring you no real advantage.

- Take care of your health. An illness now could prove very wearisome.

Advice to the Wayfarer

Your life has a solid basis, but at the moment there is no real chance for success. Take time, wait and think over what the best way is for you. Above all, take no risks. **Dharma**: the early kings gathered their virtue. When the new spring roused them, music bounded out.

● 77 NOISE AND SMOKE

Fine-sounding promises
turn out to be noise and smoke.
Honor and wealth are out of your reach now,
so cherish your friends and follow their advice.

Waxing Moon: Emerging Yang

This is the source of energy and power, the origin of sexual drives.
Use it to unfold your plans. Rouse things, help them emerge and
flower. Free yourself and play.

Season: Spring & the East *Element*: Wood

Symbols: Thunder, Wind & Wood

Life Cycle: birth & childhood

---

*If you can free yourself of the clatter of worldly fame and fortune, this
can be a very fertile time. You are rich in your friends.*

What Can and Cannot Happen

- Your household is disordered. There are simmering tensions
  that could soon break out into real difficulties.
- Don't count on business success or an increase in profits for
  now. Creative energy is on the rise.
- Don't be disappointed if your plans for a significant relationship
  fall through.
- If you want children you must be patient, for it will take quite
  a while.
- Don't go to court, for the judgement will go against you.
- If you are sick, the recovery will be slow.

Advice to the Wayfarer

Now is the time to stop and wait. Let things renew themselves. Above all, don't try to make your own wishes prevail. Don't just trust your own judgement. Ask your friends for advice. **Dharma**: the greatest illusion is that you are alone.

• 78 NOT TOO HOT, NOT TOO COLD

> You shouldn't heat chilly water
> until it turns to steam.
> Not too hot, not too cold –
> warm water is just the right thing.

Full Moon: Yang in Action
**Everything grows, matures and ripens, vigorous and effective.
Unfold and complete your plans and watch them bear fruit. Care
for the children.**
***Season*: Summer & the South *Element*: Fire**
***Symbols*: Brightness & Warmth**
Life Cycle: adults, parents

---

*Balance the activity of this very busy time and watch all your hopes
bear fruit.*

What Can and Cannot Happen

- You are happy and harmonious in the shelter of your family.
  There is no reason to think this will change.
- Follow through with your business plans. Everything is very
  promising and will bring a considerable prize in the end.
  Creative energy is at your service.
- If you want a significant relationship, now is the time. It will be
  very happy.
- If you are expecting a child, it will be a son.
- If you are expecting guests, get things ready. They will soon
  arrive.
- If you are involved in conflict, appeal to a friendly third person
  for a peaceful reconciliation.

- Unless you have very good reasons to the contrary, a change of home will greatly benefit you.
- If you are sick, don't worry. You will soon be on your feet again.

Advice to the Wayfarer

You have never really chosen which way you want to go, but now you are confronting a choice. Don't go to extremes. The middle way is always the best and the most secure. Be sure to seek the advice of an influential friend. **Dharma**: free yourself from joy and sorrow and the great fortress will rise in your heart.

• 79 GO YOUR OWN WAY

Do only what is real.
Plans that aren't real are doomed to disaster.
Each person has his or her own principle,
so don't be influenced by other people's bad advice.

)

Waning Moon: Emerging Yin

This is the time to harvest. It will bring insight as well as profit.
Reap and gather your crops. Conserve your energy and nourish the
spirits. Honor the experienced.

Season: Autumn & the West *Element*: Metal

Symbols: Mists & Heaven

Life Cycle: the Elders

---

*Concentrate your insight and discriminate illusions carefully. Then you
reap the reward of truth.*

What Can and Cannot Happen

- Your household seems to be in order. Take care that difficulties don't erupt and plunge you into discord.
- Be careful in business affairs. Do your job calmly and carefully so that no one can deceive you. Gather and concentrate creative energy.
- All the signs say you will not begin a significant relationship in the immediate future.
- If you are expecting a child, it will be a daughter.
- If you are planning a trip, be ready to make unscheduled stops.
- Solve conflicts in a friendly fashion through the arbitration of a third person.

- Don't change your home now. You have everything you could wish for here.
- If you are sick, don't worry. You will soon be well.

Advice to the Wayfarer

Above all else, do what the Goddess of Compassion tells you to do. Give up your wish-dreams and get acquainted with reality. Think about your next step and see if it is really possible. If it is, then get to work and don't be sloppy. Work until you are ready for success. **Dharma**: if you see the Buddha in the road, ignore the Buddha!

• 80 CLEAR HEAVENS

> Sun and moon shine in the clear heaven.
> A powerful, highly placed person
> guides you through all obstacles.
> Everything acts to further.

Dark Moon: Yin in Action
Put things to the proof, submit to the ordeal, separate wheat from chaff by divination. This is the time of the seed and the hidden pearl. Rely on the Ancestors' wisdom.
Season: Winter & the North *Element*: Water
Symbols: Stream & Mountain
Life Cycle: ancestors, the Old Ones, the dead

You have found the treasure hard to attain — clarity, insight and compassion. The Protectors will smile on you.

What Can and Cannot Happen

- Be happy about the joy in your family. Don't do anything to disturb it.
- Your business is going well. Work hard and sooner or later you will have a considerable income. Find the hidden creative energy.
- If you want a significant relationship, your wish will soon come true.
- If you want an heir, you will soon have one.
- If you must go to court, the judgement will be in your favor.
- If you want to change your home, go through with your plans. The change will be much to your advantage.
- If you feel ill, seek advice but don't worry unnecessarily.

Advice to the Wayfarer

Pursue your goal from beginning to end. Be strong and consistent. Someone who knows the right way will be there to help you. You can trust what the future will bring. **Dharma**: call on the Protector and the seas of temptation will soon be calmed.

• 81 WEARY TRAVELERS

In late fall
leaves fall from the oaks
and weary travelers leave like migrating birds.
Heaven will protect their journey.

Waxing Moon: Emerging Yang

This is the source of energy and power, the origin of sexual drives.
Use it to unfold your plans. Rouse things, help them emerge and
flower. Free yourself and play.

Season: Spring & the East *Element*: Wood

Symbols: Thunder, Wind & Wood

Life Cycle: birth & childhood

---

*Turn away from the busy world and a new spring, blessed by heaven,
emerges within for you and your loved ones.*

What Can and Cannot Happen

- Destiny has given you a happy and peaceful family life. Be thankful.
- New business possibilities are in the works. If you pursue your goals you can bring in a very significant profit. Creative energy is rising.
- Your significant relationship is happy and harmonious. There is no reason it should change.
- If you are expecting a child, be careful. You should be under a doctor's care.
- If you can't resolve conflicts out of court, don't worry. The judgement will be in your favor.

- If you want to change your home, do so. It will definitely be to your advantage.
- If you are sick, don't worry. You will soon be well.

Advice to the Wayfarer

You are a bit discouraged and unhappy at the moment. Whatever the reason, you really shouldn't bother. Heaven has you under her care. Your mood will gradually lighten. When you have the fresh energy and courage to carry out your plans, your efforts will be rewarded. **Dharma**: return to the source and the way.

• 82 THE WATER LILY AND THE FIRE

The scorching heat of a forest fire.
Through a happy chance, the lily survives the blaze.
It is not only spared from the flames,
but new leaves and tendrils sprout on each stem.

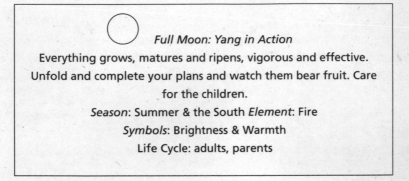

Full Moon: Yang in Action
**Everything grows, matures and ripens, vigorous and effective.
Unfold and complete your plans and watch them bear fruit. Care
for the children.**
Season: **Summer & the South** *Element*: **Fire**
Symbols: **Brightness & Warmth**
Life Cycle: adults, parents

*You emerge from a frenzy of activity renewed and invigorated. All your
plans bear fruit.*

What Can and Cannot Happen

- There is tension in your family and you are part of the cause. Clear things up as soon as you can.
- Be careful in all your business transactions. Your competitors are on your heels and are trying to steal your success. Creative energy is at your service.
- If you are expecting a child, let a doctor watch over the pregnancy and birth.
- If you go to court, the judgement will probably go against you.
- Don't change your home. A new place will only bring new difficulties.
- Be careful of your health. If you are sick, see a doctor immediately.

Advice to the Wayfarer

Your turbulent situation will calm down quickly and your precarious situation will become secure. Someone will come to your aid. Expect help and advice. Don't worry, everything will work out well in the end. **Dharma**: we learn who we are through our suffering. Watch for the spirit's return!

• 83 MOON MONTH

The moon waxes and wanes in natural rhythm.
On the third or fourth of each month, the feeble half-moon
glimmers,
On the fifteenth, the full moon shines.
Round and full in the night sky, it lights the entire heavens.

) *Waning Moon: Emerging Yin*
This is the time to harvest. It will bring insight as well as profit.
Reap and gather your crops. Conserve your energy and nourish the
spirits. Honor the experienced.
Season: Autumn & the West *Element*: Metal
Symbols: Mists & Heaven
Life Cycle: the Elders

---

*Hidden in the rhythm of things is the clarity you need. Concentrate
your insight and let it come into view. Then you will reap the rewards.*

What Can and Cannot Happen

- Your household and family are under a spirit's protection.
  Destiny has given you a happy family life.
- Your business ventures will be successful, particularly in spring
  and summer. Gather and concentrate creative energy.
- If you want to begin a significant relationship, you must be
  patient. The realization of your desire will be delayed.
- If you are expecting a child, it will be a daughter.
- If you are in conflict with someone, settle the differences
  through compromise and arbitration.

Advice to the Wayfarer

Although it seems that your relationships are strained, this is not really the case. Everything is developing quite naturally. So be patient and wait until the right time comes. When the moon is full, everything will proceed without a hitch. **Dharma**: waxing and waning, living and dying, the way is always the way.

• 84 THE FALLEN WORLD

Virtue is spoiled through evil actions.
Corruption and greed spread unhappiness.
The drunken man doesn't know where to turn.
All is lost and the soul sorrows.

Dark Moon: Yin in Action

Put things to the proof, submit to the ordeal, separate wheat from chaff by divination. This is the time of the seed and the hidden pearl. Rely on the Ancestors' wisdom.

Season: Winter & the North *Element*: Water

Symbols: Stream & Mountain

Life Cycle: ancestors, the Old Ones, the dead

A great disaster and a special fate. Can you find the treasure hidden in this darkness?

Advice to the Wayfarer

As long as nothing is pressing, don't do anything. All your affairs stand under an unlucky star. Take precautions to avoid unhappiness. Think about what you can do for your family. Be careful in everything you do. Above all, beware of false friends. Let things go if you have the slightest doubt. You could easily fall into a trap. Find the hidden creative energy. **Dharma**: retreat and nourish your virtue.

• 85 THE WAY TO THE SUMMIT

On the way to the summit,
the clouds part.
The way
is hidden in the mists.

(*Waxing Moon: Emerging Yang*
This is the source of energy and power, the origin of sexual drives.
Use it to unfold your plans. Rouse things, help them emerge and
flower. Free yourself and play.
Season: Spring & the East *Element*: Wood
Symbols: Thunder, Wind & Wood
Life Cycle: birth & childhood

If you can free yourself from the clouds of confused feeling, this can be a very fertile time.

What Can and Cannot Happen

- Relations are strained in your family. You must do something about it.
- You are running your business without putting in much effort. If you really exerted yourself, you could significantly increase your earnings. Creative energy is on the rise.
- Although you want to begin a significant relationship, hold back for now. There is little chance of immediate success.
- If you go on a trip, count on encountering obstacles.
- If you are expecting a child, it will be a daughter.
- Try not to go to court, for the odds are against you.

- If you change your home, you will discover a whole new world to explore.
- If you are sick, be careful or the illness will become chronic.

Advice to the Wayfarer

It's clear you must do something, but you don't know which way to go. The signs are good, however, so take this opportunity seriously. Because you are basically an active person, it won't be too hard. **Dharma**: be of one mind. When the Two become One, the way will open.

• 86 A Lightning Bolt

Jump off the highest mountain like a bolt of lightning.
The world will notice you.
The Emperor will give you a position,
and a poor man will become a millionaire.

Full Moon: Yang in Action
Everything grows, matures and ripens, vigorous and effective.
Unfold and complete your plans and watch them bear fruit. Care
for the children.
Season: Summer & the South *Element*: Fire
Symbols: Brightness & Warmth
Life Cycle: adults, parents

---

*A special fate. Take action. Like the sudden flash of enlightenment you
will burst upon your world.*

Advice to the Wayfarer

Like fresh flowers on a balcony in spring, this is a special fate. You
can do anything you wish to do and won't be forced to share with
anyone. This is the best fate that you could wish for. You will have
everything you want, for yourself and your family. Be happy and
give others a bit of your abundance. The signs are excellent and
you are surrounded by luck, but remember that everything won't
simply fall into your pocket. You have to give something yourself.
Creative energy is at your service. **Dharma**: a lightning bolt,
sudden glory. The open sky seen in the mind.

• 87 CLIMBING THE MOUNTAIN

A mountain climber works his way to the peak.
The sun is setting, a critical situation.
He prays to the heavens
and finds refuge among the rocks.

)) *Waning Moon: Emerging Yin*

This is the time to harvest. It will bring insight as well as profit.
Reap and gather your crops. Conserve your energy and nourish the
spirits. Honor the experienced.
Season: Autumn & the West *Element*: Metal
Symbols: Mists & Heaven
Life Cycle: the Elders

---

*The darkest hour before the dawn. Concentrate your insight and shelter
in the rewards it brings.*

What Can and Cannot Happen

- There is little agreement and a lot of egotism in your family at
  the moment. A bit of consideration for the needs of others
  would go a long way.
- Be very careful in professional matters, particularly in business
  transactions. Gather and concentrate creative energy.
- Keep your plans for a significant relationship on hold. Now is
  no time to give up.
- If you want to have children now, be patient and seek a doctor's
  advice.
- Don't go to court. The judgement will go against you.
- If you feel ill, do seek advice. It might be a serious disorder.

Advice to the Wayfarer

Although things don't look too rosy at the moment, don't be worried. As soon as you can get to work, the obstacles will vanish. Don't depend on anyone. Go your own way. Think over each step carefully and you won't go wrong. **Dharma**: the Wise One is flexible as water and always finds the way.

• 88 THE WOODEN TIGER

A ferocious wooden tiger
stands before the door
you wish to enter,
but he harms no one.

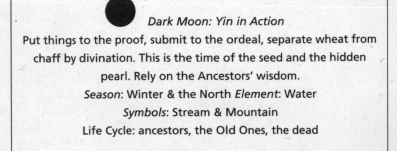

Dark Moon: Yin in Action
Put things to the proof, submit to the ordeal, separate wheat from
chaff by divination. This is the time of the seed and the hidden
pearl. Rely on the Ancestors' wisdom.
Season: Winter & the North *Element*: Water
Symbols: Stream & Mountain
Life Cycle: ancestors, the Old Ones, the dead

*Find the treasure hidden behind the constant play of illusions
and emotions.*

What Can and Cannot Happen

- Your household is full of conflict and you are in danger of being caught in a scandal. You must clear this up!
- Expect devious attacks in business by those who want to prevent your progress and harm your endeavor. Find the hidden creative energy.
- There is not much hope for a significant relationship now.
- If you are expecting a child, be careful and seek advice. It can only help you.
- Don't go to court, for you will lose your case.
- If you want to change your home, think it over carefully. It will bring you no advantage.

- If you are sick, see a specialist. Your illness could be quite complicated.

Advice to the Wayfarer

You are calm and cautious, so the wooden tiger won't fool you. Don't worry. Simply go on your way. It won't be hard to do this, for you are basically a realist. **Dharma**: fear, desire and ignorance are the roots of illusion.

• 89 THE HIDDEN JADE

Who can look
at a simple stone
and see that it hides
a piece of pure jade?

Waxing Moon: Emerging Yang

This is the source of energy and power, the origin of sexual drives.
Use it to unfold your plans. Rouse things, help them emerge and
flower. Free yourself and play.

Season: Spring & the East *Element*: Wood
Symbols: Thunder, Wind & Wood
Life Cycle: birth & childhood

Hidden in your simple situation is a new birth of joy and wonder.

What Can and Cannot Happen

- Happiness and satisfaction reign in your family. There is no sign the situation will change.
- Your business is running smoothly and will bring you a considerable profit someday. Creative energy is on the rise.
- Your plans for a significant relationship will succeed and bring you real happiness.
- If you are expecting a child, it will be a son.
- If you are expecting guests, make ready. They are on their way.
- You can go to court with confidence, for the judgement will go in your favor.
- If you want to change your home, it will work only to your advantage.

- If you are sick, don't worry. You will soon be on your feet again.

Advice to the Wayfarer

A very influential person will offer you help. Accept this aid and you will very quickly attain your goal. There is no reason to be dissatisfied with your situation. The future offers you every happiness. **Dharma**: the Protector can give you insight into what is real and what is not real. Just ask.

• 90 A MESSAGE FROM DESTINY

Destiny has a special message for you.
It is approaching
like jewel–laden ships
that reach a safe harbor.

○ *Full Moon: Yang in Action*

Everything grows, matures and ripens, vigorous and effective.
Unfold and complete your plans and watch them bear fruit. Care
for the children.

Season: Summer & the South *Element*: Fire

Symbols: Brightness & Warmth

Life Cycle: adults, parents

A special fate. Your hour has come. Spread the fruits to all.

Advice to the Wayfarer

Destiny has chosen someone to stand behind you and help you.
Take courage! You need go only a little further and success will fall
into your hand. Creative energy is at your service. Your hour has
come and wishes you have long cherished will come true. Prepare
with great care and use your abilities to help bring you to the goal.
Don't be discouraged by minor obstacles, for your stars are very
favorable. Let that give you the courage to face the minor obstacles that may arise. Show yourself full of self-confidence and faith
in your future. **Dharma**: clean the mirror of the mind. What is
there? The empty sky.

• 91 Change Your Fate ✦

Be ambitious to distinguish yourself.
Change your ways and destiny will reward you.
A wide street stands open.
You sail the boundless seas, carried by friendly winds.

🌙 *Waning Moon: Emerging Yin*
This is the time to harvest. It will bring insight as well as profit.
Reap and gather your crops. Conserve your energy and nourish the
spirits. Honor the experienced.
Season: Autumn & the West *Element*: Metal
Symbols: Mists & Heaven
Life Cycle: the Elders

---

*A special fate. Take hold with both hands. Concentrate your insight and
reap the rewards of diligence and effort.*

Advice to the Wayfarer

Whatever you want, go to work and be persistent. You have
drawn an extraordinary fate. But don't be too bold! Gather and
concentrate your creative energy. Think of your fellows, who
aren't as lucky as you are. All the help that you give them will be
returned to you one day. **Dharma**: at this very moment you are
the Buddha, if you can only see it.

● 92 Use Your Knowledge

Put your knowledge
to good use.
You will be rewarded
with honor and fame.

Dark Moon: Yin in Action

Put things to the proof, submit to the ordeal, separate wheat from
chaff by divination. This is the time of the seed and the hidden
pearl. Rely on the Ancestors' wisdom.

Season: Winter & the North *Element*: Water

Symbols: Stream & Mountain

Life Cycle: ancestors, the Old Ones, the dead

---

*You have found the hidden treasure. Prepare yourself to put it to use for
the happiness of all sentient beings.*

What Can and Cannot Happen

- There is profound peace in your household. You are safe in the
  bosom of your family.
- Your business will enjoy wide-ranging success. If you stub-
  bornly pursue your goals, you will make a considerable sum.
  Find the hidden creative energy.
- If you wish a significant relationship, it will be harmonious.
- If you want an heir, one day you will have one.
- If you must go to court, the judgement will be in your favor.
- If you want to change your home, don't delay. A new place will
  bring many advantages.
- If you are sick, don't worry. Your illness won't last long.

Advice to the Wayfarer

Depend on yourself now. Your courage and your ability to accomplish things without being discouraged will become more and more valuable. Stand firmly on both feet and fear nothing. **Dharma**: the Goddess says that without compassion and the desire to serve others, we are less than the beasts and the stones.

• 93 PHOENIX FEATHERS

> Even a sparrow does not respect a phoenix
> whose feathers are soaked in the rain.
> One day the heavens will clear
> and her soggy feathers will change back to a cloak.

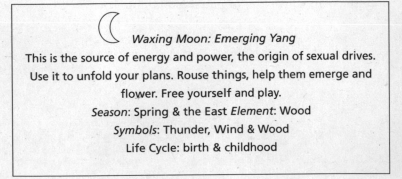

Waxing Moon: Emerging Yang

This is the source of energy and power, the origin of sexual drives.
Use it to unfold your plans. Rouse things, help them emerge and
flower. Free yourself and play.

Season: Spring & the East *Element*: Wood

Symbols: Thunder, Wind & Wood

Life Cycle: birth & childhood

If you can free yourself from rage and envy, this can be a very fertile time.

What Can and Cannot Happen

- Your household is restless. Beware. This could break out into conflict.
- Your business is not running smoothly, but you will soon overcome the difficulties. Creative energy is on the rise.
- Be careful about a significant relationship. Don't rush into things. Be sure this is really the partner for you.
- Don't go to court. The odds are against you.
- Don't change your home now. It will not help.
- If you are ill, see a doctor.

Advice to the Wayfarer

In unhappy times, you must expect humiliation. When the rainy days end, you will win back all your honor. At the moment, you are oppressed by people who are happy to have something to hold against you. Hold back. One day the tide will turn and you will be free to do what you want to do. **Dharma**: free yourself from the compulsive love of glory and honor.

● 94 THE TRUE GENTLEMAN

The true gentleman
holds himself aloof from the mob.
The noble tones of the harp are rightly treasured
only by those who know them.

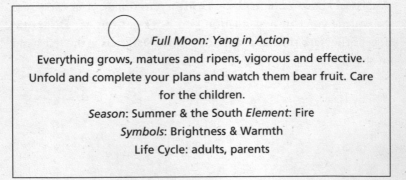

Full Moon: Yang in Action
Everything grows, matures and ripens, vigorous and effective.
Unfold and complete your plans and watch them bear fruit. Care
for the children.
Season: Summer & the South *Element*: Fire
Symbols: Brightness & Warmth
Life Cycle: adults, parents

*Your inner world ripens and comes to fruition. Guard it carefully from
the poison of negative emotions.*

What Can and Cannot Happen

- Your household is running smoothly and there will be no abrupt changes.
- Beware of accidents, particularly on trips.
- Business offers no chance to go forward and selling off assets won't really help. Profits will not improve immediately, but creative energy is at your service for future plans.
- If you want a significant relationship, be patient. Your plans will take a long time to mature.
- If you are expecting a child, it will be a daughter.
- If you expect guests, they will soon arrive.
- Don't go to court. Settle unofficially through compromise.

- Be careful of your health, for an illness now could last a long time.

Advice to the Wayfarer

You can expect help from a friend who knows and treasures you. Hold yourself aloof from others for now. That way you can resolve your problems and difficulties. Don't overestimate your capacities or you may get into a situation you can't get out of. **Dharma**: accept the dark time and walk on alone. Darkness is the left hand of the light.

• 95 CARRY ON!

Be ambitious
and strive to make a living.
The king will honor you
And bless you with rewards.

) *Waning Moon: Emerging Yin*

This is the time to harvest. It will bring insight as well as profit.
Reap and gather your crops. Conserve your energy and nourish the
spirits. Honor the experienced.

Season: Autumn & the West *Element*: Metal

Symbols: Mists & Heaven

Life Cycle: the Elders

Concentrate your energy and insight to make a great single-pointed effort. Then you can reap the rewards.

What Can and Cannot Happen

- Your household would be in a better state if you spent more time with your family and occupied yourself with their problems.
- Your business will prosper only if you really exert yourself. You have the chance to significantly increase your income. Gather and concentrate creative energy.
- Congratulations! Your significant relationship is very happy and all the signs say it will continue that way.
- If you are expecting a child, the birth will probably go smoothly, though it is always wise to seek advice.
- If you plan to go to court, pull back immediately. The judgement will go against you.

- Don't change your home now. It would only work to your disadvantage.
- If you are sick, don't worry. You will soon be well again.

Advice to the Wayfarer

Pursue your ambitions and persevere to the end. It is never too late. Be diligent and endure. One day your efforts will be richly rewarded. **Dharma**: the Great Protectors fight courageously to defend the way of the real.

• 96 THE SEVEN-STORIED PAGODA

A seven-storied pagoda
Stands on the summit of a hill.
From wherever you look,
it glitters and glows in the evening sun.

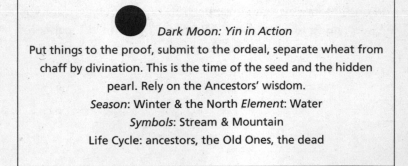

Dark Moon: Yin in Action

Put things to the proof, submit to the ordeal, separate wheat from chaff by divination. This is the time of the seed and the hidden pearl. Rely on the Ancestors' wisdom.

Season: Winter & the North *Element*: Water

Symbols: Stream & Mountain

Life Cycle: ancestors, the Old Ones, the dead

You have found the treasure hard to attain. Now let it purify your wishes and emotions.

What Can and Cannot Happen

- There is dissension in your family. Be careful not to stir up the fires.
- You will be a winner in the battle for earthly goods. Any business you turn your hand to will be successful. Find the hidden creative energy.
- You care for your partner very much, so commit yourself now. The union will be harmonious and happy.
- You will soon be happy at the birth of an heir.
- If you are waiting for guests, get everything ready. They will soon appear.
- It is meaningless to go to court. Settle this conflict through a third party.

- If you want to change your home, do so. You will be even more successful in a new place.
- Have no cares about your health. If you fall ill, you will soon recover.

Advice to the Wayfarer

You have nothing to worry about. Destiny has success in store for you on all fronts. Beware of vanity and conceit, however, for you are very susceptible to them. **Dharma**: dwell in the palace of noble intentions and wish-fulfilling jewels.

• 97 CANDLELIGHT AND SHADOW

> The candlelight throws shadows
> that dance on the wind,
> like flowers
> scattered on green fields.

Waxing Moon: Emerging Yang

This is the source of energy and power, the origin of sexual drives. Use it to unfold your plans. Rouse things, help them emerge and flower. Free yourself and play.

Season: Spring & the East *Element*: Wood

Symbols: Thunder, Wind & Wood

Life Cycle: birth & childhood

Free yourself from the strife of conflicting emotions and this will be a very fertile time indeed.

What Can and Cannot Happen

- Put your household under the care of heaven. Things are smoldering beneath the surface and strife could break out any moment.
- Luck is with you in business, but be very careful of your partners. Creative energy is on the rise.
- Your significant relationship is happy and will stay that way.
- If you are expecting a child, all will go well for mother and baby.
- Settle conflicts out of court, for you will have no luck before a judge.
- Don't change your home now. A new place would be very difficult.
- If you are sick, don't try to cure yourself. See a doctor now.

Advice to the Wayfarer

Your way is laid out by destiny, and it will be good to you. It could bring fame and fortune, but the choice is yours. Destiny opens the door, but you must walk through it. Think over the steps you must take. When you reach a decision, don't let anything turn you from your path. **Dharma**: compulsive desire is a bad companion. Take the Protector with you on your way.

● 98 THE CARELESS BIRDS

Like a careless bird
that plunges into the net,
you are trapped.
There is hardly a chance for escape.

◯ *Full Moon: Yang in Action*

Everything grows, matures and ripens, vigorous and effective.
Unfold and complete your plans and watch them bear fruit. Care
for the children.

Season: Summer & the South *Element*: Fire

Symbols: Brightness & Warmth

Life Cycle: adults, parents

---

*Caught in a swirl of activity and ambitions, you are vulnerable to your
enemies. Wake up, Noble One! Pull yourself together.*

What Can and Cannot Happen

- Mistrust and sorrow shadow your household. Purify things with tact and insistence as soon as you can.
- Be careful in all business transactions. The outlook is not good and you could suffer losses. Creative energy is at your service.
- Your significant relationship is on the knife's edge. It could fall apart at any moment. Try sincerely for reconciliation.
- Don't go to court, for the judgement will surely go against you.
- Don't change your home. The best place for a new beginning is right where you are.
- Don't take sickness lightly. Go to a doctor at once.

Advice to the Wayfarer

People are not well disposed toward you at the moment. Be very careful that you don't fall into a trap someone has laid for you. Keep calm and draw things out, but don't give up your plans. The time is not far away when you will be free again to develop them. **Dharma**: he who sows the wind shall reap the whirlwind; he who lives by the sword shall die by the sword. There is no escaping this karmic law. Change now and you can be freed.

• 99 Ashes and Ruins

A rider who whips his horse and lets go of the reins
will surely stumble.
A man who sets his own house on fire
will find only ashes and ruins.

) *Waning Moon: Emerging Yin*
This is the time to harvest. It will bring insight as well as profit.
Reap and gather your crops. Conserve your energy and nourish the
spirits. Honor the experienced.
Season: Autumn & the West *Element*: Metal
Symbols: Mists & Heaven
Life Cycle: the Elders

---

*A self-inflicted disaster is looming. Pride and greed will trap you. Wake
up, Noble One! Open your heart or face destruction.*

What Can and Cannot Happen

- Family conflict is bothering you. Give it your attention and smooth out the friction.
- You are confronting a whole range of business obstacles. If you aren't very energetic, you will be in serious trouble. Gather and concentrate creative energy.
- Your significant relationship will not be successful as long as both you and your partner always want the last word.
- Don't go to court, for the result is uncertain. Seek an out-of-court settlement.
- Don't change your home now, for it would bring no advantage.
- If an illness lingers, seek a specialist so it won't become chronic.

Advice to the Wayfarer

You are a hard worker, but you are also an egotist who ruthlessly pursues his private ends. This will hurt you in the long run, for one day the enemies you have made will have the upper hand. Bridle your ambition so you don't suffer shipwreck. **Dharma**: he who is driven by greed and ambition rolls boulders up a hill only to see them fall. Take warning! The net of your karma grows tighter.

• 100 A Sign from Heaven

Heaven gave you
an important sign.
You threw it away
and listened to a fool.

Dark Moon: Yin in Action

Put things to the proof, submit to the ordeal, separate wheat from chaff by divination. This is the time of the seed and the hidden pearl. Rely on the Ancestors' wisdom.

Season: Winter & the North *Element*: Water

Symbols: Stream & Mountain

Life Cycle: ancestors, the Old Ones, the dead

A special fate, you had the gift and refused it. Now you must search again for the treasure you threw away.

Advice to the Wayfarer

Take no action. Let things run on naturally. Wait until the situation changes. The stars are against you. Be patient, for the sun always follows the moon, and the sun is peeking over the horizon at the moment. Do nothing. Use the time to think over your situation, your household, your marriage and your business opportunities. Find the hidden creative energy. Make plans, so that you can use chances when they are offered. Find what you can do to make your significant relationship happy again. Above all, keep a cool head! **Dharma**: even the Protector cannot help a fool who throws away a priceless treasure.

Index by Number

Index by Name

FURTHER READING

The classic description of the Bodhisattva's Way is Shantideva (trans. Batchelor), *Guide to the Bodhisattva's Way of Life*, Dharamsala: LTWA, 1979. A deeply moving explication of this Way is Tensin Gyatso, The Fourteenth Dalai Lama, *A Flash of Lightning in the Dark of Night*, Boston and London: Shambala, 1994. See also Har Dayal, *The Bodhisattva Doctrine in Buddhist Sanskrit Literature*, (1932, reprint Delhi, 1970) and Kajiyama Yuichi, 'On the Meaning of the Words Bodhisattva and Mahasattva', in *Indological and Buddhist Studies: Articles in Honor of Professor J. W. de Jong*, ed. L. A. Herman et al., pp. 253–270, Canberra, 1982.

On the cult of Kuan Yin, see C. N. Tay, 'Kuan Yin: Cult of Half Asia', *History of Religions* 16, November 1976, pp. 147–177; Alexander Coburn Soper, *Literary Evidence for Early Buddhist Art*, (Ascona, 1959); *Scripture of the Lotus Blossom of the Fine Dharma*, trans. Louis Hurvitz, (New York, 1976); Henri Maspero, *Taoism and Chinese Religion*, trans. Frank Kierman Jr., (Amherst, 1981), particularly 'The Mythology of Modern China', pps. 166–171; M. Palmer, J. Ramsey, M-H. Kwok, *Kuan Yin*, London & San Francisco: Harper Thorsons, 1995; and, a truly beautiful and moving book, John Blofield, *Bodhisttva of Compassion*, Boston: Shambala, 1977.

Basic texts on Pure Land are in *Sacred Books of the East*, v.49, 1894, rpt. NY: 1965. See also Henri de Lubac, *Aspects de bouddhisme*, Paris, 1955; Marie-Thérèse de Mallman, *Introduction à l'étude d'Avalokiteçvara*, Paris, 1948; Kenneth Chen, *Buddhism in China*, Princeton: Princeton University Press, 1972 (rpt.); and entries 'Amitaba' and 'Ching'tu' in *Encyclopedia of Religion*, ed. Mircea Eliade, University of Chicago Press.

Translations, commentary and background for the *I Ching* and the *Great Treatise* are in Stephen Karcher, *Ta chuan: the Great Treatise*, New York: St. Martin's Press, 2000 and *How to Use the I Ching*, NY: HarperCollins, 2001. *Ta chuan* was the most important cosmological and spiritual document in post-Han China. Through its re-imagining of the ancient practices of the *wu* or mediums, it turned *Change* into a way of spiritual transformation.

On divination see Stephen Karcher, *The Illustrated Encyclopedia of Divination*, NY: HarperCollins, 2001; 'Oracle's Contexts: Gods, Dreams, Shadow, Language', in *Spring* 53/1992 and 'Which Way I Fly is Hell: Divination in the Shadow of the West', *Spring* 55/1994; Michael Loewe and Carmen Blacker, *Divination and Oracles*, Boulder CO: Shambala, 1981; Philip Peek, ed., *African Divination Systems: Ways of Knowing*, Bloomington IND: Indiana University Press, 1991; Maric-Louisc von Franz, *Divination and Synchronicity: The Psychology of Meaningful Chance*, Toronto: Inner City, 1980; Jean-Paul Vernant ed., *Divination et rationalité*, Paris: Editions du Seuil, 1974; and the entry 'Divination' in the *Encyclopedia of Religion*, ed. Mircea Eliade, Chicago: University of Chicago Press.

The *I Ching* is now available in many translations. Richard Wilhelm and Cary F. Baynes, *The I Ching or Book of Changes*, (Princeton: Princeton University Press, 1967) is the 'classic' English translation, now badly outdated. Richard John Lynn, *The Classic of Change: The I Ching as interpreted by Wang Bi* (New York: Columbia University Press, 1994) is a translation of the first full Confucian revision of *Change*. For those who can read between the lines it is quite frightening. Wu Jing-Nuan, *Yijing*, (Washington, D.C.: Taoist Study Series, 1991) is an interesting and usable Taoist version of the oldest parts of the text. Edward Shaugnessy, *I Ching: the Classic of Changes* (The First English Translation of the Newly Discovered Second-Century B. C. *Mawangdui* Texts), New York: Ballantine, 1996 is scholarly, interesting but unusable. I suggest my own *How to Use the I Ching*, NY: HarperCollins, 2001 and *The Classic Chinese Oracle of Change* (with Rudolf Ritsema), NY: HarperCollins, 2001, for both text and background.

Good translations of basic Taoist texts are: Arthur Waley, *The Way and its Power: A Study of the Tao Te Ching and its Place in Chinese Thought*, London: Unwin, 1934, rpt. 1977; Burton Watson, *Complete Works of Chuang T'zu*, New York: Columbia University Press, 1968; and A. C. Graham, *The Book of Lieh t'zu*, London: John Murray, 1960.

Kuan Yin is a major inspiring figure in the great novel about the *Journey to the West* to fetch the scriptures of liberation. See Arthur Waley (trans.), *Monkey*, Harmondsworth: Penguin, 1961 (excerpts) or A.C. Yu (trans.), *Journey to the West* 4 vol., Chicago: University of Chicago Press, 1977 (complete).

On thought and culture in traditional China, see K. C. Chang, *Art, Myth and Ritual*, Cambridge MA: Harvard University Press, 1983; Marcel Granet, *La pensée chinoise*, Paris: Albin Michel, 1934; J. M. M. de Groot, *The Religious*

System of China, 6 volumes, 1892–1910, rpt. Taipei, 1967; Henri Maspero, *China in Antiquity*, trans. Frank A. Kierman, University of Massachusetts Press, 1978; J. Paper, *The Spirits are Drunk: Comparative Approaches to Chinese Religion*, Albany: State University of New York, 1995; and Benjamin Schwartz, *The World of Thought in Ancient China*, Cambridge MA: Harvard University Press, 1985.